The author was born in Cheshire, educated at the Wirral Grammar School, served on a destroyer in the Mediterranean, read history and archaeology at Cambridge University, and worked there as a research assistant. After experience on numerous excavations in Britain, including as assistant director and director, in 1961 he went to Nigeria, where he spent ten years excavating and on fieldwork. In 1971, he moved to the University of New England in Australia, founding the archaeology department there and later becoming its foundation professor. He returned to Nigerian fieldwork in 1978 and 1981 and subsequently excavated in Egyptian Nubia and Uganda. He also contributed to Australian historical archaeology and founded the journal Australasian Historical Archaeology. He is a Fellow of the Royal Anthropological Institute, a Fellow of the Society of Antiquaries, a Fellow of the Australian Academy of Humanities, MA (Cantab), D.Litt (UNE), and holds the Order of Australia.

Graham Connah

ARCHAEOLOGY AT TWO AUSTRALIAN UNIVERSITIES 1971 TO 2023

AUSTIN MACAULEY PUBLISHERS™

LONDON • CAMBRIDGE • NEW YORK • SHARJAH

A CIP catalogue record for this title is available from the British Library.

ISBN 9781035845408 (Paperback)
ISBN 9781035845415 (Hardback)
ISBN 9781035845422 (ePub e-book)

www.austinmacauley.com

First Published 2024
Austin Macauley Publishers Ltd®
1 Canada Square
Canary Wharf
London
E14 5AA

Table of Contents

Preface

This book is a history of my time at the University of New England and at the Australian National University. It is primarily about research and teaching archaeology, but it also describes the personal background of this work in order to provide the context in which it was done. In addition to myself, many other people are part of the story, interesting people, many now deceased but who deserve to be remembered. They include both academic staff and non-academics as well as those outside the universities who contributed in various ways to the institutions. A university is a community, but it is also part of a larger community on which it depends for its success. Overall, the book is a tapestry of the times, that is, of times that are no longer with us.

The contents of the book are extremely varied, concerned with Australian shell middens, the ruins of historical buildings in Australia, traditional farming in Nigeria, salt-making in Uganda, urbanisation in Egyptian Nubia, technology in China, but all these subjects have something in common. They are about our becoming human; they help us to understand who we are and how we came to be the way we are.

Over the years, governments have interfered more and more in universities and the way that they are run, emphasising science and technology and giving less attention to the humanities, the subject that makes us human. Politicians are so obsessed with war or the threat of war that these are often their main concerns. The humanities are regarded as less relevant. This inevitably influences the students at universities and in the over fifty years covered by this book I must have had contact with some thousands of them.

I like to think that their study of archaeology has given them a more balanced and more humane view of the world. It should also have given them something else; a capacity for critical thinking, an ability to analyse evidence. Dealing with archaeological evidence, it is constantly necessary to ask what it tells us and how we know this. Epistemology is vitally important; how do we know what we think we know? In a world dominated by dictators who distort the truth and create 'fake news', the truth is increasingly important and increasingly elusive.

The book has no dedication because the people described in it are, in a sense, its dedication. It has been a pleasure to write about them.

Graham Connah

Canberra

July 2023

List of Figures

29. Winterbourne, Cutting I completed 1976
30. Winterbourne, excavation staff at lunch 1976
31. Winterbourne, research assistant Mike Rowland 1976
32. Mrs Jane Richards for whom the house was built, 1976
33. 'Ohio', that housed staff of Winterbourne excavation 1976
34. Frank Choate at Grafton Airport and Cessna 1976
35. Bora ring and colonial cemetery at Tucki 1976
36. The Great Wall of China, near Beijing 1977
37. Stone elephant, Beijing, with tour member, 1977
38. Bronze bell from Xi'an, with James Bowen, 1977
39. UNE tour of China, at Mao Tse Tung's birthplace, 1977
40. Krakatoa from *Kota Singapora*, Beryl in foreground 1977
41. Farming tools for firki soils, Sangaya 1978
42. Pointed stake to make holes for masakwa seedlings Sangaya 1978
43. Masakwa ready for harvest, Sangaya, with technical assistant 1978
44. Masakwa in grass-lined storage-pit, Sangaya 1978
45. Farmhouse near Chwilog, Lyn Peninsula, Ian in doorway 1978
46. Graham's 1960s yawl in 2011 at Longhope, Orkney
47. Lower North Row 1960s Longhope house, 2011
48. The book about the Borno research, written in 1978
49. John Mulvaney late in life
50. Aerial photograph of Bagots Mill site before excavation 1977
51. Bagots Mill as Bagot might have intended it
52. Bagots Mill, inside wheel-chamber completely excavated 1980
53. Bagots Mill, Alan Connah on the wheel-chamber wall, probably 1980
54. Reddestone Creek excavation completed, July 1980
55. Reconstruction of Diprotodon
56. Bill Cameron, local historian of Glen Innes
57. Graham Connah in Mount Beef Tunnel 1979
58. Graham Connah in Mount Beef Tunnel with fall 1979
59. Mount Beef tunnel, pick-marks 1979
60. Aerial photograph of the track, Pindera Downs, western NSW 1980
61. Aerial photograph of fish-traps, Bayley Island, Queensland 1982
62. Aerial photograph of Gostwyk woolshed, Armidale, NSW 1980
63. Aerial photograph of Trial Bay Gaol, NSW coast 1982
64. Borno fieldwork team 1981

1.

Introduction

This is an account of work and life in Australian archaeology from the 1970s to 2023. In early October 1971, with my wife Beryl and our three children, Alan, Ian and Sarah, respectively eight years, two years and two years old, I flew from London to Sydney, Australia, breaking our journey for one night at Singapore, at that time more 'traditional' and smaller than it has since become. The next day we flew on to Sydney in the first 'Jumbo' Jet that I had seen and perhaps the first to go into service.

I have often been asked why I decided to go to Australia. The truth is that I wanted a job and, as a specialist for many years in West African archaeology, I had little chance of finding one in Britain. There was only one post in African archaeology at a British university and that was held by Colin Flight at the University of Birmingham. Britain seemed to have rejected its imperial history and African colonial past, along with the government and commercial participants of that time, many of whom had been sincere in their efforts during the naivety of African independence in the 1960s.

Some of my contemporaries had gone to jobs in American universities or museums but these had become scarce by 1971 and my lack of a PhD made it unlikely that I would get any employment there. Earlier I had no money for the necessary three or four years of study for a PhD, later I had no time for it. In the 1960s, I registered for a PhD at the University of Ibadan in Nigeria but abandoned work on it after several months because of the time demands of my Research Fellowship employment at that university.

In the 1980s, I solved the problem by acquiring a D.Litt. for my published books, a qualification superior to that of the PhD. As for Britain, in the 1970s an obsession with itself seemed to have developed in universities and, indeed, generally in the country. Subjects like the archaeology of Cornwall could create employment but not Africa.

Before leaving Britain, I had visited Grahame Clark at his house in Cambridge. As we sat in his garden, he told me that he had visited the University of New England at Armidale, which he said was a pleasant place. However, he advised me to develop and keep contacts with the few prehistoric archaeologists in Sydney, Canberra and Melbourne, although I doubt if there were any in Melbourne at that time, John Mulvaney having recently moved to the Australian National University in Canberra. This was advice that I was to find wise and tried to follow.

I also visited Thurstan Shaw, who happened to be on leave from Nigeria in Cambridge. After lunch in Clare Hall, where we met for the last time in some six years, I told him that at the University of New England, I would be joining the Department of Ancient History. Shaw had been a Classics student at Cambridge in the 1930s and had changed to the Department of Archaeology and Anthropology, attracted by the excitement of its research and teaching at that time, compared with the boredom of Classical Studies. His response to my information was predictable: "My God," he said, a remark that I was to remember as an indication of the task that I would have to take on.

So it was that I found myself, a specialist in West African archaeology, teaching archaeology at an introductory and general level, such as the evidence for the origins of agriculture and the development of cities. This was as a lecturer, not a senior lecturer as I had been at the University of Ibadan. I had come down a level but was determined to get back to the senior lecturer as soon as possible. Before leaving Britain, I had spent three weeks living in Cripps Court at Selwyn, my college at Cambridge, reading as widely and as much as possible in archaeology, as a preparation for what I would have to undertake.

Also, before leaving Britain, I bought myself the best single-lens reflex camera that I could afford and an electric typewriter. I intended these to replace facilities that had been provided at the University of Ibadan but I doubted would be so available at the University of New England.

2.

Beginning in Australia

We arrived in Sydney on 9 October 1971 and flew on to Tamworth airport, which looked desolate and little-used. After a short time there, we flew on to Armidale, where the airport seemed a little more lively than that at Tamworth. We were met there by Isabel McBryde, who was the only archaeologist at the University of New England. I had met her briefly many years before, at the Iron Age settlement site at Barley near Cambridge. This was when I was surveying and planning the excavation there on the morning after the 1959 May Balls. She had been doing a certificate course in archaeology at Cambridge, following a degree at Melbourne University supervised by John Mulvaney.

Subsequently, Isabel was appointed to a lectureship at the University of New England in 1960, showing the innovative thinking of that university at a time when there were few such appointments in Australian archaeology in the country. She had responded by undertaking an extensive fieldwork programme on Aboriginal prehistoric sites in the New England region.

This had been aided by financial support from the university and elsewhere and by the participation of other members of the university in an initial excavation at Seelands, a rock shelter near the upper Clarence River, west of Grafton. Other excavations and fieldwork had followed and Isabel had acquired a Land Rover, the most successful four-wheel-drive vehicle of the 1960s, to enable access to many of the prehistoric sites that were difficult to reach. She had also been very successful in getting undergraduate and honours students to participate in the research.

As a result, by 1971 she had been promoted to Senior Lecturer and then to Associate Professor and both she and archaeology had earned wide respect in the university. Her research also earned her a PhD at the University of New England in 1966, which became the basis of a book about the prehistory of New England that was published by Sydney University Press in 1975. Indicative of the status she had achieved within the university, by the time I arrived in 1971, she had become an elected member of the University Council, the governing body. In a university where women were in the minority amongst senior academic staff, this was a remarkable achievement.

When I arrived at the university, things had changed. The Land Rover had been replaced by an Alfa-Romeo and Isabel was living with her parents on a small property at the western edge of Armidale, where she kept a horse for riding. Formerly, she and her family appear to have lived in Melbourne, but she had been born in Fremantle, Western Australia, in 1934. Her father was the retired captain of a passenger ship that had operated between Melbourne and Fremantle but ceased to do so because of the growth of air transport during the 1960s. By 1971, he was suffering from memory-loss but his wife was looking after him as well as she could.

Isabel had taught prehistory as the third part of a first-year course that also included Greek and Roman history, with the possibility of the eventual creation of a separate Department of Prehistory. In addition, she had taught the subject at second, third and Honours level, as well as doing postgraduate supervision. It was in this overall context that I had been appointed to assist her.

At UNE, as the university was most often called, I was to teach prehistoric archaeology, mainly at a first- and second-year level. In preparation for this, I spent the summer vacation, after arrival, writing a series of first-year lectures and preparing material for second-year and third-year practicals, as well as for use at a more advanced level. The third and final teaching term had ended for the year, but I helped with marking and invigilating examinations, including those for subjects other than archaeology.

At the first exam, I was paired with Jim Ryan from the English Department, then a Senior Lecturer I think. He was a rather excitable man, known to other staff as 'Jungle Jim', apparently because of his appearance when he returned from three weeks excavating with Isabel McBryde in 1961. The exam was at a time when the student unrest in the USA and Britain had eventually reached Australia.

At the end of the exam, the subject or subjects of which I forget, Ryan insisted that we collect all the papers from the students before they were allowed to leave the room because otherwise, some students might take their papers with them and later claim that they had been lost by us or by the markers. Their tactic was at least better than smoke bombs in the exam room, as was also happening at that time and which would probably have sent Ryan into hysterics if it had occurred.

Ryan's contribution to the university was to continue till his retirement and beyond, in particular editing various publications, including the Armidale and District Historical Society Journal and Proceedings. I found him rather pedantic but his contributions to the university were undoubtedly significant.

When I arrived at UNE, Isabel suggested that I develop a research programme in historical archaeology, then a new field but one that had not yet had much attention in Australia. However, it was 1974 before I had the sense to take her advice. Instead, from 1972 to 1974, I excavated and did other fieldwork on Aboriginal coastal shell middens in the lower Macleay Valley. I only changed my attention to historical sites in 1974–1975 (**Figure 1**).

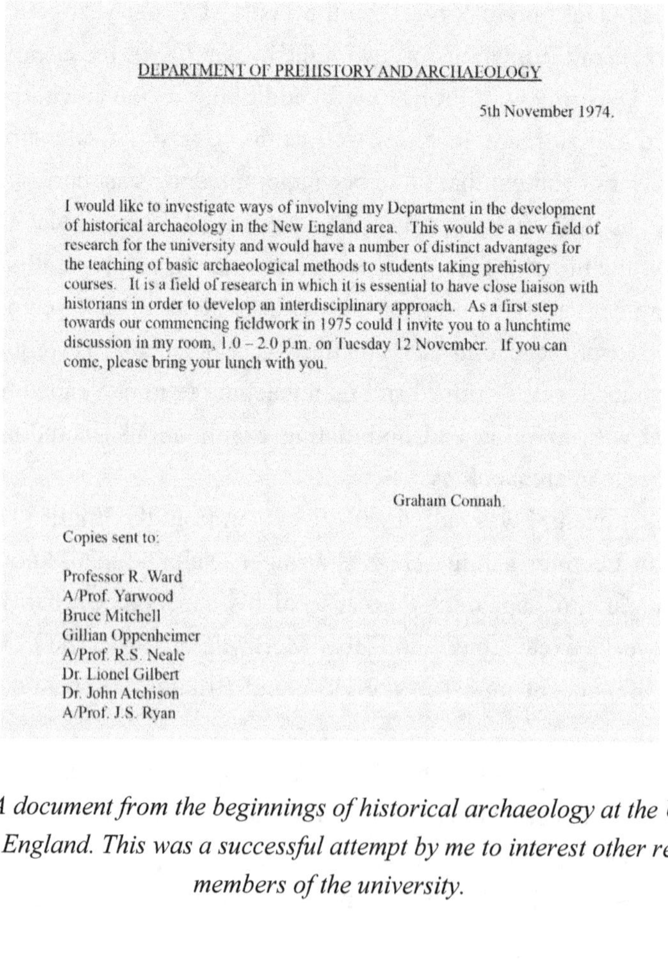

DEPARTMENT OF PREHISTORY AND ARCHAEOLOGY

5th November 1974.

I would like to investigate ways of involving my Department in the development of historical archaeology in the New England area. This would be a new field of research for the university and would have a number of distinct advantages for the teaching of basic archaeological methods to students taking prehistory courses. It is a field of research in which it is essential to have close liaison with historians in order to develop an interdisciplinary approach. As a first step towards our commencing fieldwork in 1975 could I invite you to a lunchtime discussion in my room, 1.0 – 2.0 p.m. on Tuesday 12 November. If you can come, please bring your lunch with you.

Graham Connah.

Copies sent to:

Professor R. Ward
A/Prof. Yarwood
Bruce Mitchell
Gillian Oppenheimer
A/Prof. R.S. Neale
Dr. Lionel Gilbert
Dr. John Atchison
A/Prof. J.S. Ryan

Figure 1. A document from the beginnings of historical archaeology at the University of New England. This was a successful attempt by me to interest other relevant members of the university.

3.

Housing and Other Problems

On our arrival, after a couple of days at the Zebra Motel, in Armidale, we were accommodated in an apartment within a building, parts of which the university rented for new arrivals. This was near the then teachers training college. We were allowed six weeks to find somewhere else to live, but this proved difficult because there was little available at that time. We could have rented an apartment but with three young children, we needed a house.

After a long search, we found an advertisement in 'Smiths Weekly', a duplicated news sheet that the university produced. This enabled us to lease an old wooden house, probably built cheaply in the late nineteenth century, 147 Markham Street, near the centre of Armidale. It was in very poor condition indeed and very cold in the one winter (1972) that we spent in it. I fixed sheets of clear plastic over the inside of the windows, but they made little difference to the inside temperature.

The only heating was an open fire in one room if I remember correctly. This we fed with wood offcuts purchased from a local sawmill. It was so cold in the winter that icicles hung from the bath taps some mornings. The toilet and laundry were outside and I could see spots of light through the ceiling and roof above our bed. The other houses in the street were better but occupied by people of lower economic status than us who must have been puzzled by the presence of someone from the university, with his family. The neighbours on one side had several sons who made life difficult for Alan.

On the other side, there was a teenage girl who was friendly but had parents who took no interest in her, indeed her father seemed to be an alcoholic. Our house had poor fly screens if any at all and a low point for us was when we found the remains of the Christmas turkey swarming with blowfly maggots on Boxing Day 1971. It was one of the only two occasions that I saw Beryl weep. Inevitably, the house caught fire and was burnt down in 1978 when students were living in it. It was rebuilt but probably without much improvement.

After our move from Nigeria, our finances were very stretched. Isabel's mother must have realised our difficulty because she regularly brought us fruit and vegetables, a kindness that we much appreciated. The university paid us a removal allowance, but it did not cover the expenses of a journey as long and as complicated as ours had been. In Nigeria, we had sold our car before leaving, but because of the recent civil war, the lack of new cars, the shortage of spares and its age of seven years, our car was worth little. Even the £150 Nigerian that we got for it could not be taken out of the country.

Eventually, a Dutch friend in Ibadan, Peter van Meer, got it out for us because he worked for the United Nations. Our finances were made worse by the university not paying my first wages until six weeks had passed. When I asked for a bridging loan from our new Australian bank (I think the Commercial Bank of Sydney), it was refused by the manager, who failed to understand our situation.

Things got so bad that I was reduced to straightening old bent nails to do odd jobs in the house. Fortunately, some people were much more helpful and gave us two particularly good pieces of advice. These were to take out medical insurance (many years later I still have my HCF policy) and to join the NRMA (a New South Wales motoring association that would come to your aid if you broke down). I remained a member of the latter until I gave up driving in 2021.

At the end of my first year at the University of New England, I attempted to get promoted to Senior Lecturer, as I had been at the University of Ibadan. My application was rejected perhaps because I had only recently joined the university.

The Markham Street house remained a problem and I had to purchase a few things: a hammer, a small axe (a 'hatchet' in Australia) and some gardening tools such as a spade and a rake. The house, I discovered, did have one advantage, its back garden. After I had cleared up the broken glass and other rubbish, it proved to have fertile soil, because the centre of Armidale was on deep valley sediments that must have been worked over by gardening occupants of the house for a century or more. I was able to grow several vegetables. Beetroots were particularly successful, the largest that I have ever grown before or since.

Meanwhile, Beryl could not work, because she had to look after Sarah and Ian, now over two years old. However, Alan was able to attend the

'Demonstration School', where his neglected education was rectified by some good teachers, including Kent Mayo and a woman whose name I forget.

One of our worst problems, however, was the non-arrival of our 'loads' from Nigeria, which contained essential household items and my books, although we had given away as much as possible before leaving.

Eventually, they did arrive, after a nine-month journey on a French ship aptly named 'Le Kangarou'. I then made repeated enquiries to the Sydney agents and discovered that our possessions had been put into storage there without me being informed. It was insisted that I pay a storage fee but I refused and at last, they were delivered to our house in Armidale. Everything had been packed in strong wooden boxes, but a few items were damaged by water, probably because at some stage the boxes had been left in the rain. A cherished framed photograph of Beryl's parents was partially damaged and in 2023 it still reminded us of these matters.

4.

Rosemary Lucas to the Rescue

Then came a big change in our domestic situation. One afternoon in the autumn of 1972 I was peeling potatoes in our kitchen, when a dishevelled, middle-aged woman appeared in the doorway, having apparently just walked into the house, as witnessed by Alan who was there.

"I hear you're looking for a house," she said. Her name was Rosemary Lucas and she had a property called 'Sunray' about 10 kilometres to the west of Armidale. She raised Charolais cattle there, was unmarried and ran the property on her own. We went with her to see the place. It was a sound, wooden house of about 1900 vintage, standing in a fenced enclosure in the middle of a grassy paddock.

I immediately said that we would have it and the rent was reasonable. Rosemary, it seemed, was living or prepared to live, in a barn a little way from the house. The house had a number of rooms, an open fireplace, electricity and water, but only an outside laundry and toilet (a 'dunny' in Australia) with a pan.

After years of the Nigerian bush, this was alright with us and once a fortnight I dug a hole in the paddock behind the house to bury the contents of the pan, with Alan assisting me. The house also had a garden, the part in the front with a few shrubs that I clipped from time to time. After a while, I built a chicken-run near Rosemary's barn and the chickens in it supplied us with eggs. Altogether, we were very happy with our move and particularly with Rosemary as our only neighbour.

Rosemary ran her property, as the Australian saying goes, 'on the smell of an oily rag'. She had little capital, except the land and the cattle and depended on bank support. Consequently, everything that she had was old and worn-out. Her only transport was a battered, dirty and rusty 'utility'. A little way up the hill near our house was a large heap of wood, onto which every piece of scrap went for potential reuse, nothing was wasted. I spent the morning of Christmas Day 1972 trying to start a petrol-driven water-pump on the nearby Saumarez Creek, that supplied water to a corrugated galvanised-iron tank on the top of the hill near the house.

From there, it was gravity-fed to the house and other parts of the property. I had never seen a pump like it, it looked as if it dated from the 1920s or earlier and it probably did. It took me a long time to get it going and on a later occasion, I failed to do so.

Rosemary did everything possible to belong to a non-money economy. I once found her repairing one of her fences with the help of a man that I did not know. When I remarked on her ability to pay him, she responded 'He owes me'. In other words, she had done some sort of favour for him and expected a favour in return. The man might have been one of the 'us-ers', several brothers from the northern edge of Armidale along the New England Highway. They lived together in a rundown house surrounded by junk, looked after by their sister. I discovered that they were known as the 'us-ers' because that was how they referred to themselves.

It was through Rosemary that I came across Stan and Charlie Fardell, also from the struggling part of rural society. They had a small property west of Armidale. At that time, pork was expensive in the shops and they raised pigs which they sold in Tamworth. Often when I met them, they would tell me; 'pigs is good' and because pigs will eat almost anything, the two brothers must have done fairly well. They had two houses on their property but lived in only one of them, so they decided to rent the other one to students from the university.

However, there was a snag, I think that it lacked hot water, so they got an electrician to install a water heater. When it came to paying him, they offered him a pig instead of money. He refused to take it, insisting that he wanted his money, but eventually, he left with two pigs, for which he would have had to arrange butchering. The two brothers were different, Charlie was well built but Stan was very thin and it was he who ploughed up part of our land when we moved to 'Longhope', a house of our own, after leaving 'Sunray'.

Both had died by the time I returned to Armidale on a visit in late 1995. I mainly grew potatoes at 'Longhope' but on one occasion when visiting them I noticed that some of the vegetables in their garden had gone to seed. I remarked that they should have harvested them earlier. One of them replied that they were keeping them for seed the next year. Like Rosemary Lucas, they belonged to the make-do economy. Overall, we enjoyed our life at 'Sunray', it was a quiet rural setting and we became acquainted with the few other people who lived in the area. Alan spent a lot of time with Rosemary and learnt something about life on the land, as Beryl and I also did. He was able to camp during some nights in the back paddock, depending on the weather, in a tent that we must have bought for him.

Some mornings Beryl and I were woken up early by possums in the roof of our house, making a noise as they returned from their night's foraging. Beryl's friend from New Zealand (**Figure 2**), through whom we had adopted Sarah and Ian, visited us for a week or so in the summer of 1973 and complained about the 'rats' in the ceiling, so eventually I employed a man to remove the possums. Because they were protected, they could not be shot.

Figure 2. 'Sunray', summer of 1973-1974, myself, our children, Beryl and Peggy Wilkes from New Zealand. Rosemary's house is in the background.

The summer of 1973 had a lot of rain. Out for a walk with Beryl's New Zealand friend, we had to shelter on one occasion beneath the Saumarez Creek bridge adjacent to Rosemary's property. At about this time, the creek flooded and we were briefly cut off from outside contact. Overall, our time at Rosemary's place taught us a lot about life in rural Australia.

Meanwhile, Rosemary did try to improve things. She re-seeded some of her land, got a central-European inventor to fit one of his automatic gates at the entrance to her property and even installed a septic tank for our house, but of course, it was an old corrugated-iron water tank recycled. Limited capital made her very thrifty. As she said, regarding her cattle: "You sell when others are buying but buy when others are selling."

Eventually, she did sell a small part of her land to Betty Hall, a local vet, to build a house on and Rosemary's property was subdivided after her death, at an unknown date but possibly about 2010.

Rosemary was a fund of information about other occupants of rural Saumarez. Near her property was a man called Ron Cherry, who was a drover, making a living by moving animals from place to place. Rosemary recorded how on one occasion he was trying to load an obstinate cow onto a truck with his wife pushing from behind and twisting its tail, a common technique. However, the animal retaliated by releasing a flood of manure over his wife and her clothing. When she complained, he told her not to worry and said, "It's just grass and water."

I know little about Rosemary's background except that her father had died when she was a teenager or slightly older. At about that time, she had won a travelling scholarship to visit farming in the US or Canada, I cannot remember which. I assume that she had inherited her property from her father. She had a brother, but he worked for Australia Post, I think as a postman. A steady wage must have been more attractive than the uncertainties of life on the land. She called the property 'Sunray', but I do not know if that was her choice or her father's.

For a while, she had another property, called 'Sunray 2', that she ran with a man called Grahame Browne. It was north of Armidale, somewhere near Guyra and in a different environment from Sunray 1. This was presumably to make agistment possible, a common farming strategy in Australia that allowed stock to be moved to suit short-term changes in weather conditions such as droughts or floods. She gave a lot of thought to such matters.

Rosemary had not married but in 1989, at the age of 55, decided to do so. She married a man a bit older than herself, who was also in farming. The wedding was unbelievable. It took place in the tiny, wooden, century-old Anglican church at Saumarez, near her Sunray 1 property. The church was too small and some of the numerous guests had to stay outside where, although it was a late afternoon in September, it snowed!

Cars got bogged in a scene that became chaotic, but worse was to follow. The wedding reception was little short of bizarre. A large marque and barbecues had been set up on Rosemary's property, hired from a firm that usually attended to the requirements of agricultural shows. However, this was no sunny afternoon but a frigid evening that grew ever colder as time passed.

By now, the snow had stopped but it was bitterly cold. Nevertheless, an amazing number of people attended the reception, showing how wide Rosemary's contacts were. The marque was only loosely-fastened on the side where the barbecues were and there was no heating for the guests, who sat at long tables.

Added to the woes of the guests was the lateness of the food, which took hours to appear, but in the best Australian tradition, the alcohol was abundant. The result was that most of us got increasingly drunk as it grew colder and colder. It was no occasion for cold beer but there was lots of wine and, when my supply began to run low, Betty Hall appeared by my side with a bottle of red and said, "Here, you might be needing this."

I had been asked to propose the toast to the bride and groom and by the time that I did so, as I said later, the top half of me was frozen and the bottom half was intoxicated. Altogether it was a night to forget rather than to remember as had been intended. Beryl and I eventually got home, by then Watson Avenue, Armidale, about midnight.

5.

Life at 'Longhope'

Nevertheless, we were very grateful to Rosemary and we were happy during the time that we lived in the house at Sunray. However, we wished to buy a house of our own, rather than to continue paying rent. By now, our two houses at Longhope, on the island of Hoy, in the Orkneys, had been sold, I think, by Jackie Groat, who had also probably handled the sale of my yawl and dinghy.

With the proceeds and with a mortgage through the University of New England, we looked for a house and eventually decided to buy one about 15 kilometres west of Armidale along Bundarra Road. It was on the top of the Dividing Range, with a fine view west. It had just been built, by a man called Lawman, who was not a builder but had subcontracted the work to others. He had a flooring business in Armidale and traded as 'Lawman the Floorman'.

We bought the house and its approximately 14-acre plot. We named it 'Longhope', in memory of our Orkney days and we moved in during March 1974, Rosemary assisting with her battered utility to transport heavy items. While at Rosemary's, I had made a chest-of-drawers, a desk and a set of dining chairs, from New Zealand *Pinus radiata* kits and these went with us, along with a Nigerian carved chest and a Nigerian carved coffee table that Beryl had bought during her first tour in 1960.

We also had beds for the children but not one for ourselves. So, we ordered a double bed, but it had to come from Sydney, I think and Armidale proved, as so often, its inability to obtain and deliver, while Beryl and I slept on a mattress on the floor for six weeks.

The house stood towards the top of a steep hill, was single-storied and had four bedrooms, a study, a living room and kitchen combined, a pantry, a laundry, a bathroom, an ensuite and a garage. It faced north with a front veranda. Because of difficulties with its construction, it was too near the western boundary fence, beyond which was the house of another family, called Christian. Frequent interruptions in my university study made it almost impossible to mark assignments and exam papers or to prepare lectures, practicals and seminars there. So, I did a lot of such work at home in the evenings or at the weekends and often worked till nearly midnight. Consequently, I was told that 'Longhope' became known locally as 'the house with lights'.

However, I tried to spend Saturdays with Beryl and the children. In addition, there were many other things to do. After some confusion, I got postage delivered to a box that I put at our gate from the road. I also improved the drive from the gate to our house and got Stan Fardell to plough part of our property, where I planted potatoes and some other vegetables. These grew well one year when the rain was good, but badly in another when it was not. In addition, I got a chicken coop built and stocked with 20 or so hens, the legal limit for a household. They supplied us with eggs.

For a while I kept two or three geese, till we ate them, the fate also of the hens when they got too old to lay, although by then they were sometimes inedible. The house had an oil heater in the living room but no other heating, so eventually we installed a wood-burner with tiled sides and I assembled a small sheet-iron shed purchased in Armidale, to store firewood, that I cut myself or purchased locally. A similar but slightly larger shed that I put together had a concrete floor and housed garden tools, a lawn-mower and other things.

Jobs at 'Longhope' were done over some years. The biggest was the purchase of a large wooden shed from a high school in Armidale, who advertised it for sale to anyone who would remove it. I employed a man to do this and to transport it to 'Longhope', where he built a slightly smaller shed with the recycled materials. His girlfriend, a student of mine, helped him to put on the corrugated-iron roof, which I think was done with recycled sheets but with new fastenings. The shed was quite high, so we built a loft at one end for storage purposes.

About this time I bought a boat in Port Macquarie and towed it to 'Longhope' with Alan, but it proved a disaster. I sailed it only once, on Dumaresq Dam and found that it was too big for me to handle in the limited space of the dam. Then, stupidly, I tried to reduce the sail area by sawing off part of the mast but never got any more of the job done. The boat remained unused for years in the shed, gathering dust and was only disposed of when 'Longhope' was sold in 1985. I cannot remember whether I sold it or simply gave it away.

More successful was Alan, who built himself a tiny shed on the highest part of our land, the south-east corner. I think that he slept up there occasionally. His shed was made of surplus materials from rebuilding the big shed. With Ian's help and possibly Sarah's as well, he also built a low terrace wall west of the garage to prevent erosion, using some of the many basalt 'floaters' lying on the surface of our property.

We were also given a Sennon goat, a placid white-coated animal, by Iain Davidson. He had kept it for some time but wanted to get rid of it when he married his first wife, presumably because she did not like it. The goat was called 'Rumpelstiltskin' or something like that. We mated it once and, with Betty Hall's assistance, it produced an offspring which later we ate. Gio Andreoni, of the UNE Italian Department, who lived near us, demonstrated his hunting skills by killing, skinning, gutting and turning it into meat cuts ready for cooking.

Another goat that somebody left with us had obviously been mistreated and proved impossible to approach, but Iain Davidson's goat was a placid animal that provided us with milk for some time and later died of natural causes. We also looked after several plastic dustbins for Iain Davidson, in a distant corner of our property. These contained various animals that he was rotting down, in order to add their bones to our archaeology identification collection at UNE. Earlier attempts to do this had caused a problem of smell in the Faculty of Arts building when done in our workroom there and maggots invaded one of the lecture rooms when the rotting animals were transferred to the roof of the building.

Many things were done at 'Longhope'. I purchased a 22 single-shot bolt-action rifle and taught the children how to use it safely, firing at a target. Firearms were not required to be licenced at that time and accidents caused by ignorance could occur. We got a dam dug in a downhill corner of our property and equipped it with a petrol-driven water-pump that could feed water up to a corrugated-iron tank near the house.

This was water for the garden, but I also had a similar tank put adjacent to the big shed to collect water from its roof and eventually, I installed a pipe that enabled this water to top-up the underground tank beneath the house. This, in turn, had an electric pump that automatically supplied water for use within the house. All this concern with water should be seen in the context of the late 1970s, which were years of poor rainfall and drought.

Before we bought the house, I had got the builder to turn half of the double garage at the western end of the house into a study for me. Eventually, I got a small second-hand wood-burner installed in the study because it was so cold in winter and this necessitated the construction of a chimney. I was fortunate enough to find a bricklayer who still knew how to build one and he and I did it together. Another minor job was my construction of a stile over our fence with the Christians, to replace the long walk down our drive, along part of the road and up their drive. Stiles, although common in England, seemed to be unknown in Australia.

Other things happened while we lived at 'Longhope'. We held student parties in the house that were well-attended. The adjacent Bundarra Road, which was gravel and only had a bitumen surface towards the end of our time at 'Longhope', caused a spectacular roll-over car accident close to our gate. When we and Mr Christian went to investigate the outcome, we found that the contents of the car scattered on the road included a set of bagpipes!

The driver was luckily unhurt. Drought caused a build-up of dead grass, that I got The Armidale School fire-brigade to clear with a controlled burn. An attempt to do the same myself was nearly a disaster when the fire got out of control and I was only saved by the help of a neighbour from across the road. Another problem at 'Longhope' was the lengthy journey by a school bus that our children had to endure, inevitably bullied by the older ones present.

Beryl and I rented the house to an American academic visiting the university, while we were on study leave in Cambridge during 1978. During our 1983 study leave, also in Cambridge, we let Mike Morwood and his wife and daughter live in the house; I think rent-free, on condition that Alan could also be there during vacations from UNE. This was during his first year at university, which was spent at UNE before he moved to the ANU in Canberra. Unfortunately, Alan found the arrangement difficult.

Our return in 1979 from study leave marked a watershed in our lives. We had sold our VW Campervan before going away and we now bought a Holden Kingswood, with a powerful 4.2-litre V8 engine. The campervan had been underpowered and I needed a car that would get me to Sydney, Melbourne and Canberra for work purposes when required and to the coast for family holidays at other times. I also sold my University of Ibadan international superannuation and used the money to pay off our house mortgage. We still had an old Ford Cortina as well as the new Holden and we kept this going as a second vehicle for several years.

At about this time, I also decided to sell 'Longhope' but it was December 1985 before I managed to do so. By then, Alan was away at university in Canberra and Ian and Sarah were constantly needing transport to activities in Armidale, an inconvenient distance away. We sold to a woman called Shakespeare, I think, who worked for the UNE administration.

For years, we took brief holidays at various places on the north coast of New South Wales, in the week before Christmas when the academic year had ended and at some other times. Latterly, it was Yamba to which we usually went. In 1982, we were more adventurous. I hired a motorboat on the Clarence River. We travelled the navigable length of the river for a week, from the estuary to a little above Copmanhurst, although it rained frequently and the river was in flood towards the end of the time (**Figures 3 and 4**).

Figure 3. The hired boat at anchor on the Clarence River. The five of us lived on it for a week while we explored the river. 1982.

*Figure 4. The dinghy provided with the hired boat, with Alan,
Ian and Sarah in it. 1982.*

6.

Back in Armidale and Move to Canberra

We bought a single-storey house in Watson Avenue, north Armidale, I think number 16 and moved in just before going to the coast for a pre-Christmas holiday in 1985. Two removalists assisted us but that very evening one of them was killed by a train on a level-crossing at Glen Innes, a type of accident that has been too frequent in New South Wales over the years. He had been on his way home after helping us to move.

Our new house had been built in the late 1960s or 1970s and was only a short journey to the university and other facilities, Alan was now at the ANU, studying part-time while working to support himself. Ian finished school in 1987 and went to the Maritime College in Tasmania to train as a merchant navy officer, funded by us for the first year but later with a scholarship. Sarah left home in 1987, and later went to Charles Sturt University in Bathurst, where she graduated as a schoolteacher.

Beryl and I lived alone in Watson Avenue until I retired in early 1995. We then moved to Canberra, living for about three months in a house at Chisholm, that we had owned for roughly five years as a rental investment. In about April 1995, we sold it and bought a larger house in Holder, Weston Creek, No 2 Warner Place. I moved to Canberra because the libraries were numerous and good and because I had a year as a research fellow in the Humanities Research Centre at the ANU.

After that, I became a research fellow for 15 years in the Anthropology and Archaeology Department of the School of General Studies. The latter names were changed during this time, as the ANU altered its organisation. I continued to write but worked at home when I could no longer visit the ANU because it became difficult to walk. I sold my car in February 2021 because I was able to use it less and less.

A routine visit to OPSM in early 2021 showed that glaucoma had suddenly destroyed most of the sight in my right eye and that the left eye was deteriorating in the same way. Eye surgery was advised by Dr Andrew White, an eye specialist, but the developing pandemic of coronavirus delayed this for months. It was 18 June 2021 before it could be done. I remember nothing of the event or of the time just before it.

After that, I had jumbled rectangles of different colours and (separately) jumbled pieces of survey maps appear in my vision. Finally, I woke up and was told that I had been in a coma for two weeks. The reason was uncertain but was probably a complication resulting from my long-term Addison's disease. It took me several days to be able to talk or do anything and I then discovered that I had lost the use of my legs and could not even stand up by the hospital bed.

So, I remained in the Canberra Hospital for a further 10 weeks without any real improvement. Then I was transferred to the University of Canberra Rehabilitation Unit, where I stayed for (I think) five weeks, doing exercises in their gym every morning, including Saturdays and bed exercises on my own on Sundays. This got me walking again, with a 'walker' and with great difficulty, but I was very grateful to the physiotherapists there who did an excellent job. I then moved to an aged care facility, called Warrigal, in Sterling, Canberra, during October 2021, where Beryl was already. Previously she had been in another aged care facility after I was taken ill.

The above details of our domestic and family life after arrival in Australia in 1971 provide a necessary context to the following account of university matters. This concerns teaching and administration as well as research, the latter mainly about the way that it was done because the academic results have already been published elsewhere. My first lecture at UNE was a shock. I was somewhat fearful of this beforehand and rather shaken when I looked up from my notes and saw that all the students of a large first-year course were white. I had been used to black student audiences for some years and it was a long time since I had last done much lecturing in Britain.

I suppose I feared that Australian students, with the advantages of a better school education, would be 'superior' to the Nigerian students that I had been accustomed to, but I was wrong. They were different but not better. Nigerian students were highly motivated because their family or their community or a scholarship was paying their university costs. They had to succeed to justify such support. So much was this so that on one occasion there was almost a fight when

I distributed notes after a lecture but did not have enough copies for everyone. In comparison, many Australian students of the 1970s were poorly motivated and less concerned with making an effort, because they were confident of continuing family or government support.

I also ran first-year tutorials and second-year practicals, but Isabel McBryde did the rest of the second- and third-year teaching. Soon after arrival, I went on a field trip for these students of hers; she drove one university car; I drove another. The field trip was to the Moore Creek axe-factory site, just north of Tamworth.

7.

Teaching and Research at UNE

After I took over the new department in 1974 I tried to make my teaching as practical and as interesting as possible, including field trips and the involvement of students in other field activities. These included the recording of indigenous rock art in 1974 (**Figure 5**) and I got some of my students to create an 'archaeological site' for teaching stratigraphy in 1976. We excavated part of it in March 1982, although we were unable to use it later because it flooded.

As my teaching turned more and more to Australian historical archaeology in the 1980s and early 1990s, I had students investigate local historical structures or their remains. Examples included farm buildings at Saumarez, Newholme and Abington, the ruin of a steam flour mill near Glen Innes (**Figure 6**) and other ruined buildings in northern New South Wales.

This was the context in which surface recording was conducted at Lake Innes House from 1993 to 1995, prior to the excavations there. I also encouraged the study of artefacts in museums, at Glen Innes, Armidale and elsewhere, as well as an investigation of the historical Glen Innes brickworks. Our external students were involved in these activities and they were able to investigate a very varied range of subjects in the widespread locations in which they lived. To give students an opportunity to take their investigations to the publication stage, I produced a small book of some of the best of their practical studies (**Figure 7**).

Figure 5. UNE students recording indigenous rock art at Moonbi, south of Armidale, in 1974. The art was traced onto sheets of clear plastic without damage to the original. At that time, this was the best way of recording faint work. Subsequently, all such tracings were presented to AIATSIS (the Australian Institute of Aboriginal and Torres Strait Islander Studies) in Canberra.

Figure 6. Steam flourmill ruin, south of the town of Glen Innes, 1984, recorded during a student field trip.

Archaeology and the historical artefact

Edited by
Graham Connah

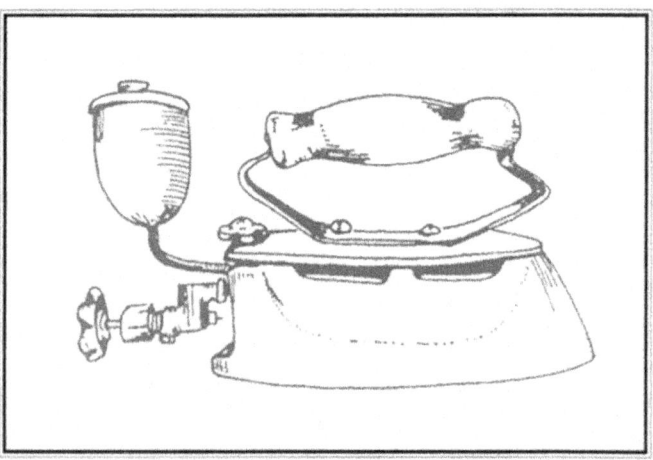

Department of Archaeology and Palaeoanthropology
University of New England
1994

Figure 7. Publication of some of the best of the student practical studies, 1994.

8.

UNE Academic Staff

John Bishop had been appointed as Professor of Classics in 1959, coming to the University of New England from the University of Edinburgh. He was a Cambridge graduate and had also been ordained as an Anglican clergyman. He had an open view of the world and regularly visited a prisoner in Grafton jail who had been imprisoned for murder.

At coffee time each morning, John Bishop sat in the Classics tearoom and talked on a wide range of subjects, 'holding court', as one member of his audience put it. He had a strong influence on the politics of the university. It was said that on one occasion, in order to get his way on some matter, as chairman of the Academic Board, he called a meeting when the Saumarez Creek had flooded and some board members could not get to the university.

By the time I arrived in Armidale, the creek had been bridged or otherwise made passable, so he could no longer use this tactic. Nevertheless, he still had a strong influence at the university. Shortly before my arrival, he combined his Classics Department with Ancient History when the History Department wanted to get rid of the latter, thus enlarging his departmental staff and in the process including Isabel McBryde in it. I was impressed by him and with hindsight, I remain so.

Of his staff, five of us eventually became professors in different universities, including myself. One or two of my earliest lectures were attended by John Bishop, who apparently approved, remarking that as he came out of the lecture theatre on one occasion, he heard a student comment that I was 'dinki di', an indication of traditional Australian approval that greatly pleased me.

Alan Henry, a Scotsman and an Associate Professor when I arrived, was Dean of Arts at that time. Henry is chiefly memorable for an advertisement he put into 'Smith's Weekly' when his Armidale house was connected to the sewer and he no longer needed a septic tank. 'Septic tank for sale', it read, 'low mileage'. He meant it and emptied it himself by hand, admitting afterwards that he had to burn the clothes that he had worn. He got a Professorship at Monash University in Melbourne and subsequently returned to Scotland.

Maurice Kelly was very helpful to Beryl and I when we arrived. He was acting head of the department at that time, as John Bishop was on study leave until the end of 1971. A young man called (Ian?) Campbell very generously lent Beryl and I an old battered Mini car while we waited for the arrival of the Volkswagen Campervan that we had ordered. The latter was fitted out very well by a firm in Fyshwick, Canberra. It had a stove, a fridge, a sink and a roof that opened. From memory, I think that it could sleep four people. John Bishop once referred to it as 'Connah's flying bedroom'.

Each department in the Faculty of Arts at UNE seemed to be a little kingdom on its own, for example, the historians had little to do with the geographers or the philosophers and contact between different faculties was rare. There was also an obsession with teaching rather than getting students to think critically for themselves. Iain Davidson was to some extent justified in calling UNE a 'super school'.

Because of my own background and because it was essential for an archaeologist, I tried to get to know as wide a range of the academic staff as possible, in different departments and different faculties. Most colourful was Jimmy Dolan, a medieval historian who visited us in the Classics tearoom on some days. He was, for instance, unimpressed when his historian colleagues introduced a course on the 'philosophy of history'. 'That's not history', he claimed, 'history is about things like the man who betrayed his city to besiegers. When the other citizens caught him, they hung him from the city walls. That's history'. All this in a broad Glasgow accent. He said that when he went to university, after the Second World War, he found that he was surrounded by clever people, but he had a solution. "I had to know more than them," he declared. Kevin Cochran, a student of mine in the early 1970s who also did medieval history, once told me that when he went to collect an essay from Jimmy after it had been marked, Jimmy commented that it was a good essay, but he could not understand why Kevin had not mentioned Bannockburn. "I did not think it mattered Mr Dolan," replied Kevin. "You did not think it mattered," Dolan exclaimed, "Here, give me the bloody thing back again, I'll take 10 per cent off it."

Later, Jimmy introduced a new course, which was about the Vikings. Taught by himself alone I suspect, it meant a lot of extra work and the day came when he was found dead on the floor of his university study, defeated by a heart attack. He deserved to be remembered. There was also Pat Watters, a New Zealand zoologist who limped because of polio in his childhood and in both name and affliction reminded me of Ikey Watters in Orkney during the 1960s. He helped me by doing a lot of display work in the Faculty of Arts Antiquities Museum. This had been started by Maurice Kelly in the 1960s, in collaboration with Isabel McBryde, but had never got beyond the pretty-objects-in-glass-cases approach. It needed to actually inform students and visiting school children and Pat Watters did this, in particular by making impressive models for inclusion in the displays. He was able to draw on his experience running the museum in the Zoology Department. Members of the university who appreciated our efforts in the museum included Bruce Mitchell of the History Department (**Figures 8 and 9**).

However, after I retired from the UNE in 1995 the museum reverted into the control of the Classics department and was run by someone who thought that the past consisted of only the Greeks and Romans. My many years of work for the museum, with endless meetings of the museum committee that I chaired and attempts to get extra funds or assistance from inside or outside the university were ignored. This made me angry but not as angry as the subsequent insulting lack of recognition of the vital work that had been done for the museum by Pat Watters, Doug Hobbs, Malcolm Able, Mike Morwood and others. Such is life, ignorance and lack of vision succeed but imagination and innovation do not.

Figure 8. Pat Watters on right, me to left, in the UNE Antiquities Museum, 1992.

Figure 9. To right Bruce Mitchell, UNE History Department, at left me, in the UNE Antiquities Museum, 1988.

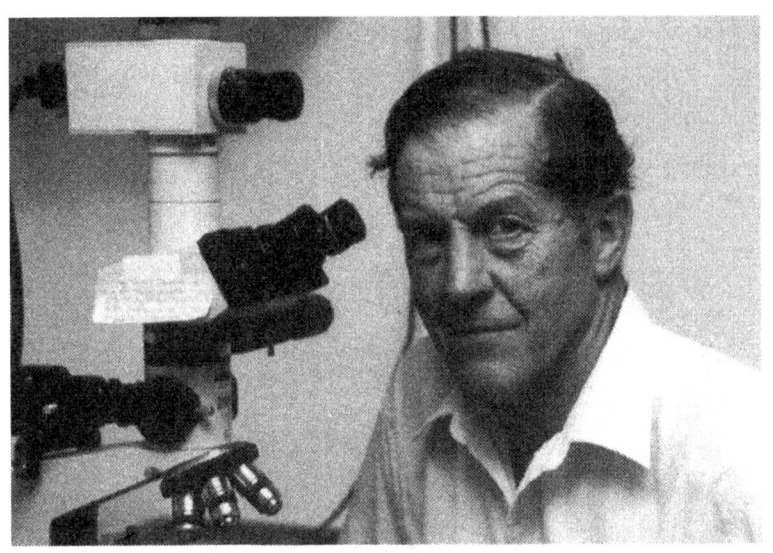

Figure 10. John Milburn,1936–1997. UNE Professor of Botany.

In addition, there was John Milburn (**Figure 10**), the Professor of Botany, a friendly man who helped me to run the Staff Club for several years until the university administration closed it down because they were unwilling to accept its independent status. Early in his career, he had worked in one of the northern countries in South America and he came to the University of New England from Glasgow University, having made his name by demonstrating that plants make noises when deprived of moisture and connected electronically.

He and I regularly had lunch together at the Staff Club, after he had played squash and we enjoyed the excellent cooking of Pat Smethurst. Milburn was working on bananas, I think in Sri Lanka, and had a fairly carefree attitude to life, riding a moped to work rather than driving a car. Eventually, he decided to build an ultralight aircraft or perhaps repair a second-hand one, despite my warnings. Inevitably, he crashed it into the ground on his very first flight and killed himself, about a year after I had retired from UNE. Also likeable was Russel Ward (**Figure 11**), a Professor of History, from South Australia and the author of a famous book, *The Australian Legend*. He said that UNE was the only Australian university that had been willing to give him a job because of his politics.

When I was promoted to Associate Professor at the end of 1976, he came to my room and remarked that it was 'too little and too late'. Another member of the History Department who deserves to be remembered was Sandy Yarwood, a friendly Associate Professor who failed to get the Chair in History when perhaps he should have got it. I suspect that he had disagreed with the university 'establishment' on various matters. However, the university did show some initiative when Sinnappah Arasaratnam, a Sri Lankan, was appointed Professor of Asian history.

Figure 11. I, Doug Hobbs and Russel Ward at the UNE launch of my Australian historical archaeology book in 1988. Doug Hobbs was an excellent graphic artist who illustrated this book and many others of mine.

There were other staff members that I found interesting and I was particularly glad that I managed to cross some of the faculty lines, communicating particularly with Professor Beadle, Professor of Botany until his retirement and with Professor Wilkinson of Geology and Professor Jack Evans of Animal Science. Other departments were less friendly, I had little contact with Organic or Inorganic Chemistry and one member of the Physics Department merely dismissed archaeology and me as 'not scientific'.

Geography was the largest department in the Faculty of Arts until the end of the 1970s but later shrank as its work was split up into various new specialised departments, such as Ecosystem Management. Nevertheless, one of Geography's remaining academic staff did prove important to me. This was Alan

Jones, a specialist in what has become known as remote sensing, who came to UNE from the University of Wales. It was with him that I got an Australian Research Council grant in the late 1970s for aerial archaeology research.

This was after I had done similar work with Frank Choate, I think of the Physics Department, who piloted many of my earlier photographic flights during the 1970s, as did Howard Creamer of the NSW National Parks and Wildlife Service, stationed in Armidale. Both were excellent pilots, reliable and safe.

The university also had numerous service departments, such as those for finance, insurance, purchasing and external studies and I frequently needed their help. Most important for me, however, was the Photography Department, run by the University Photographer, Bill Webster and later by John Field, both now deceased. They and several assistants developed and printed many photographs from my fieldwork research.

There was also a small Visual Arts Department producing video cassettes and other work. Other services included transport, maintenance, cleaning, etc., even two men who duplicated audio cassettes that were posted to external students in language courses. In fact, the university was a complex organisation of many parts. Computers and digitisation have now changed much of this and it is difficult to believe that in the 1980s there was a Computing Department run by a director who wanted computer access restricted to the 'Main Frame' and who wished to prevent academic staff from acquiring their own desk computers.

Other UNE staff who were more successful included Bruce Mitchell (already mentioned) of the History Department and his wife Jillian Oppenheimer, whose help with local history and with contacting local people in New England was so valuable to me when organising fieldwork.

Another aspect of the UNE staff needs discussion. This was its outdated treatment of women. As already mentioned, Isabel McBryde had made such an impact in the university that, by the time I arrived in 1971, she had become an elected member of the University Council, the governing body.

However, as far as I can remember, she was then one of only two women who had reached Associate Professor status in the university. Non-academic staff, such as departmental secretaries, were treated even worse. If they became pregnant, they were expected to resign. The prevailing social attitude toward women in the town became apparent to Beryl and I when we went into one of Armidale's hotels for a drink and were asked to leave or at least go into a back room. When I pointed out to the barman that bringing a woman into the bar was 'not against the law', he replied: "No, it isn't but we don't do it." Even a city like Armidale was behind the times in 1971 and rural New England was more so, as I gradually discovered. Women were second-class citizens until the reforms of the Whitlam government in the early 1970s began to change things.

However, Beryl was able to contribute substantially to our success as a family. She took on various jobs once the children were all old enough to be in school. She worked as a nurse in the Armidale Hospital and, when the New South Wales government introduced courses called 'Back to nursing' to encourage former nurses to return to the profession, it was she who ran the one in Armidale.

In the 1980s, she completed a BA Honours degree in Geography at the University of New England and was made a fellow of the New South Wales College of Nursing at about the same time. Her Honours thesis was about the care of the aged in their own homes instead of in institutions, then a new idea and subsequently she was employed to organise such care in Armidale. She even worked for a while as a carer for the aged when we were on study leave in Cambridge in 1983 and short of money.

After retirement, she worked as a volunteer for twenty five years at the Salvation Army day-care centre of Burrangiri in Rivett, Canberra and during our visits to Sweden she worked as a volunteer for the Red Cross. Her relevant qualifications were substantial and included SRN, SCM and MTD, all from Britain (**Figure 12**).

Figure 12. The Connah family in the 'pine forest' near Armidale, October 1987. Left to right: Alan. Ian, Beryl, me, Sarah.

Degree Day was undoubtedly the high point in the university year at UNE. Held early in the year, it was always on the lawn behind Booloominbah, the historic house that formed the centre of the university. Complete with a procession of volunteering academic staff (of whom I was usually one) and accompanied by a loudspeaker booming out 'Gaudeamus Igitur', it was a solemn occasion. State or Federal members for New England would be there and the Anglican and Catholic bishops of Armidale, although one of them sometimes fell asleep during the proceedings.

There would be an invited notable speaker and the Chancellor of the university would give the appropriate certificate to each graduand. Some of these would be postgraduate degrees, such as PhDs (**Figure 13**) and there would often be several honorary degrees awarded to people for outstanding achievements. We always hoped that it would not rain and in my time it never did or I do not remember it doing so.

The audience would be made up of many family members of the graduands for whom it was a day of achievement after the support they had provided, often involving considerable expense and the overcoming of other problems. I always felt that we owed it to them to put on a good 'show'. They would have come from a widespread area, some of them travelling considerable distances to be there. This was a reminder of the location of UNE and its character as a 'rural' university. All this could not occur during the COVID-19 epidemic of 2020–2022 but has since begun to revive.

In the 1970s and 1980s, the University of New England was a better university than it realised, as I told Lawrence Nichol, the Vice Chancellor, in the later 1980s. However, the Dawkins reforms at the end of the 1980s caused immense damage, which left a difficult legacy.

Figure 13. Degree Day 1996. Warwick Pearson and Claire Smith received their PhDs, with me and Beryl present and Claire's son.

I was expected to do research at the university as well as teaching and I wanted to give research as much time as possible. However, I soon had to add administration to my duties because in late 1973 Isabel McBryde announced that she was resigning and moving to the ANU in Canberra, as a Senior Lecturer in the first instance, I think.

This was on the brink of the UNE deciding to start a Department of Prehistory. The then Vice Chancellor, Alec Lazenby, an agronomist, was not in favour according to John Bishop, but the latter got the Council to pass the change while the Vice Chancellor was away. When I asked Bishop what would happen to the new department now that Isabel was leaving, he replied: "You will run it." He also got the name of the new department changed to the Department of Prehistory and Archaeology because he thought that archaeology should be mentioned and he was right.

Other UNE staff members are remembered because they were so helpful to me. The Maintenance Department were good at answering my requests for equipment needed in my fieldwork, making things especially for me on several occasions. The Transport Department were also a help with moving equipment and supplying Land Rovers or other four-wheel-drive vehicles for Beryl and I to use during our fieldwork. In addition, various parts of the UNE administration such as Finance, Insurance and Purchasing, mentioned above, as well as

Academic Records and the Dean's Office in the Faculty of Arts, were frequently of assistance.

There were two administrative problems that occupied much of my time at the University of New England. One was the difficulty of getting enough staff, a task that needed me to convince the appropriate university authorities that the department needed more. As a growing department, we struggled with inadequate staffing for many years. The other problem was the related one of having enough space for the staff to work in. The document below records the history of this matter and the changes in the location of the department that it necessitated (**Figure 14**).

DEPARTMENT OF PREHISTORY AND ARCHAEOLOGY/
ARCHAEOLOGY AND PALAEOANTHROPOLOGY

History of UNE accommodation 1974-1988 incl.

1974-77 (inclusive)	Scattered rooms in 2 corridors in Arts Building. Basement Cont.Ed. Building, replaced by part of basement of Organic Chemistry. Part of Basement of Behavioural Studies.
1978-80 (inclusive)	All above replaced by equivalent floor area, but no increase in area, in new building.
1980	Size of building found inadequate. Addition of 2 rooms at one end.
1982	Size of building again inadequate. Subdivision of Arts Lecture Room A4 and its annexation.
1986	Size of building still inadequate, following discussion of taking over part of Alluna Building, Dept. takes over Fireman's Cottage instead.
1986-7	Further 'rough' storage and workspace allocated in Clark's Farm Buildings. Very useful but value limited by lack of ventilation, heating, and toilets.

Graham Connah

Graham E. Connah,
1st March, 1988.

Figure 14. The history of accommodation for the Department of Archaeology and Palaeoanthropology, previously the Department of Prehistory and Archaeology.

9.

Excavating Shell Middens on NSW Coast

I eventually started field research during the 1971–1972 summer vacation. Here I was lucky because I was able to use a good Honours thesis by Val Campbell as a starting point. She had done this in the late 1960s, before my arrival. It was about the Aboriginal shell middens of the lower Macleay Valley and the adjacent coast. With a small research grant from the Australian Institute of Aboriginal Studies in Canberra, I was able to commence fieldwork very quickly in January-April 1972.

I was much helped by several of Val Campbell's contacts in the Macleay area, such as Mrs Blackwell, Bill Thurgood, Bob Ball, a man whose surname was Christian and others whose names have been forgotten. Bob Ball was an interesting character who lived alone on Shark Island in the estuary of the Macleay River, refusing a television set when one was offered to him and communicating with the adjacent shores by boat.

He told me that in the 1920s he had worked for John Holt in Nigeria, as what he called a 'palm oil pirate', going up the Benue River by boat each wet season to buy palm oil. It was an unexpected reminder in Australia of my years in Nigeria. The help and cooperation of these people in my midden research showed that, as in Nigeria, working with local people was very important in field archaeology.

I visited many of the midden sites and selected Clybucca 3 for excavation, a site that Campbell had sampled with an auger. I excavated there for 2 or 3 weeks in May 1972 during the vacation, using equipment of Isabel's, but I also had to hire tents from an unreliable Armidale business. These proved to be leaky during the excavation, in the wet weather that occurred. However, my Volkswagen Campervan and a portable laboratory that had previously been made for Isabel's excavations were of help. It was tough for Ian, Sarah, Alan and Beryl, because May was late autumn and fairly cold, particularly at night, but we all survived, along with several Prehistory students who had volunteered to help (**Figure 15**).

The site produced two good cross-sections of the midden (**Figure 16**) and several radiocarbon dates that were subsequently published. Later that year I returned there with one student and did a contour survey (**Figure 17**) of the main part of the midden and later still aerial photography was also done (**Figure 18**). On another but unknown date, with a student helper, I took auger samples from the swamp area on the north-west side of the midden, hoping to get waterlogged wood and seeds from it, but a member of the Geography Department with relevant skills never did the promised analysis of the samples and they were eventually lost.

The most positive outcome of the Clybucca excavation was that John Bishop was clearly impressed by the rapidity with which I inaugurated a field-research programme, arriving in October 1971 and running an excavation in May 1972. Publication of the work at the time was later supplemented with a paper by a student of mine, Graham Knuckey and myself. A magnetic survey of the midden also formed part of a study published by me, Penelope Emmerson and John Stanley in 1976.

A second midden excavation was done in May 1973 at Connection Creek (**Figure 19**). The Clybucca midden had been chosen by me because it was one of the most inland and therefore possibly early in date. The Connection Creek midden was chosen because it was nearer to the coast and might be later in date, as the sea-level fell during the early-to-mid Holocene. Again, we used tents, but they were new 12x12-foot ones that I had bought specially. Again, it rained for most of the time and, on this occasion, I had to leave part of the job to finish the following year.

However, the excavation provided more midden sections and radiocarbon dates that were published at the time. I also looked for evidence of human activity adjacent to the shell deposit and one cutting revealed this (**Figure 20**), showing that the area surrounding the middens required excavation as well as the middens. A lasting memory of the excavation was transporting the students from the site to Crescent Head to vote in the 1974 federal election, when Whitlam and the Australian Labor Party won for a second time.

Figure 15. Breakfast at the Clybucca 3 campsite, waiting for the billy to boil, May 1972. Left to right: Gillian Moon (Munday?), Murray McLachlan, Beryl Connah holding Ian Connah, Alan Connah in front, Helen Royal holding Sarah Connah. Conditions were poor.

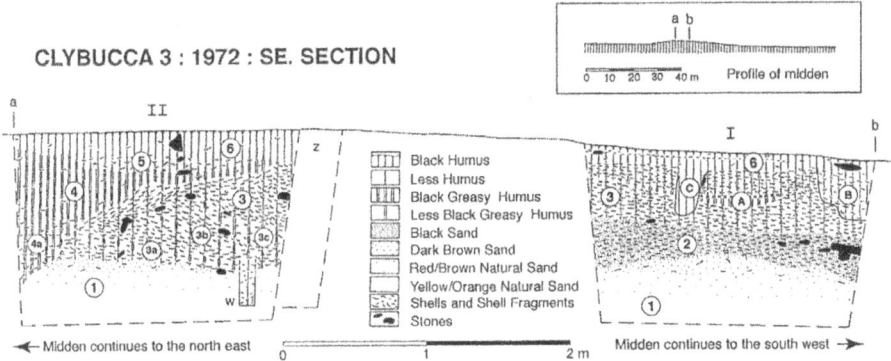

Figure 16. Section-drawings of Clybucca 3 shell midden, left to right: Cuttings II and I.

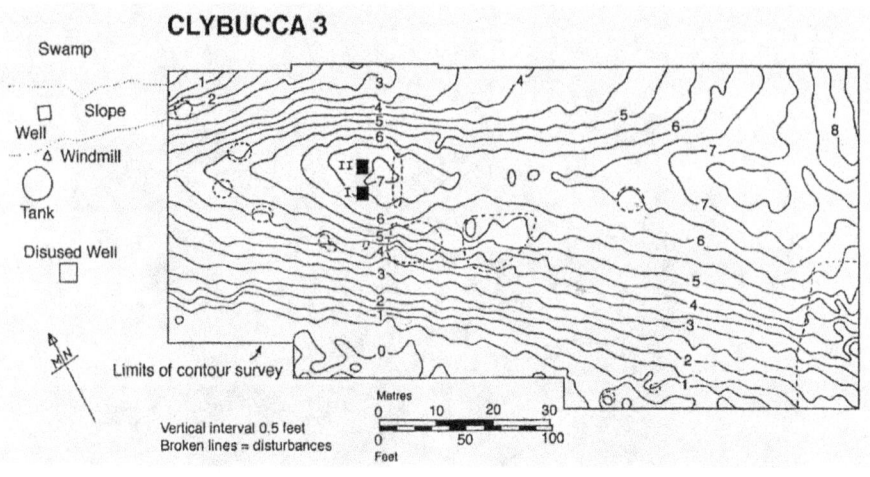

CLYBUCCA 3

Swamp

Slope

Well

Windmill

Tank

Disused Well

Limits of contour survey

Vertical interval 0.5 feet
Broken lines = disturbances

Metres
0   10   20   30

Feet
0   50   100

Figure 17. Contour plan of the Clybucca 3 shell midden, showing Cuttings I and II.

Figure 18. Aerial photograph of the Clybucca 3 midden from the south-east, August 1975. The swamp on the north-west side of the midden is surrounded by trees.

Figure 19. Connection Creek excavation in progress, with unidentified UNE Prehistory students and one volunteer. Organisation and infrastructure were better than at Clybucca in 1972. Photograph May 1973.

Figure 20. Connection Creek excavation. Cutting with evidence of human activity adjacent to the shell midden. Scale in centimetres, the arrow points to the north. May 1973.

In May 1974, excavation moved onto the present shoreline, working at Maguire's Crossing amongst the coastal dunes of the New South Wales mid-north coast (**Figures 21–22**). This presented difficulties because the loose sand at the site lost its stratigraphic integrity when walked or knelt on. To solve this problem, I placed wooden planks over the cutting to support the excavators above the excavation surface. Soon after the excavation, the site was destroyed by a storm that eroded the dunes.

However, the Maguires Crossing site provided more midden sections and radiocarbon dates that were later published. We also rescued information from Ryan's Cut near Maguires Crossing, where a midden section had been previously exposed by erosion. Similarly, we excavated at an Inner Barrier midden, a little further inland. In addition, I was asked by the New South Wales National Parks and Wildlife Service to record a section through the long Stuart's Point midden, that had been illegally dug into for commercial exploitation by someone with a backhoe. This provided us with a complete cross-section of the midden (**Figure 23**) that prevailing heritage restrictions would have prevented our obtaining otherwise.

In May 1975, I did the last and best organised of the midden excavations. This was in the same long Stuarts Point midden (**Figures 24 and 25**) of which we had recorded the illegal cross-section. During this excavation, we were able to get more radiocarbon dates and to use a Cambridge-designed flotation unit that I had acquired, to recover seeds and other botanical remains from the excavated deposits (**Figure 26**). Unfortunately, these were never studied because Peter Irish, at that time our most able student, left UNE at the end of his second year and Len Cubis, who had started work on the plant remains was killed in a car accident on the New England Highway, I think in 1978.

However, by then, I was also doing a magnetic survey and aerial photography of some of the midden sites and this work was recorded in relevant publications. Also, much later, in 2002, Wendy Beck of the UNE obtained a radiocarbon date for the shell from this midden. Previously, such dates had been mainly from charcoal. (**Figure 27**)

Figure 21. Shell midden site of Maguires Crossing excavation, before work began, May 1974. Scale in 50-centimetre divisions.

Figure 22. Maguires Crossing, excavation in progress, May 1974. The trestles were to support planks from which the excavators could work without disturbing the loose deposit.

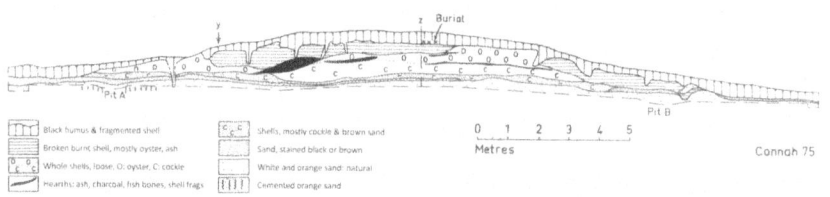

Black humus & fragmented shell
Broken burnt shell, mostly oyster, ash
Whole shells, loose; O: oyster, C: cockle
Hearths: ash, charcoal, fish bones, shell frags

Shells, mostly cockle & brown sand
Sand, stained black or brown
White and orange sand: natural
Cemented orange sand

0 1 2 3 4 5
Metres

Connah 75

Figure 23. Stuarts Point 1974. Illegal backhoe section of midden, recorded at the request of NSW National Parks and Wildlife Service.

Figure 24. Excavating Cutting I at Stuarts Point, 1975. Colour print by student.

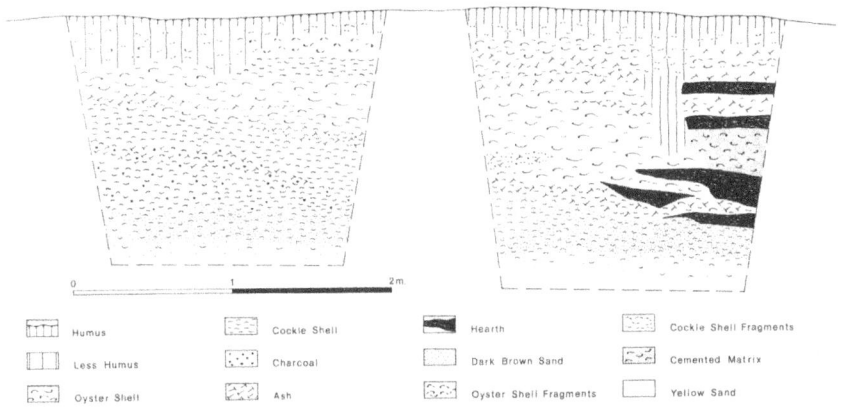

Humus	Cockle Shell	Hearth	Cockle Shell Fragments
Less Humus	Charcoal	Dark Brown Sand	Cemented Matrix
Oyster Shell	Ash	Oyster Shell Fragments	Yellow Sand

Figure 25. Stuarts Point excavation 1975, Section-drawings of, left to right, Cuttings II and I.

Figure 26. Stuarts Point excavation 1975. Cambridge flotation equipment in use to recover seeds and plant remains. Left to right: unidentified student, Peter Irish. Colour print by student.

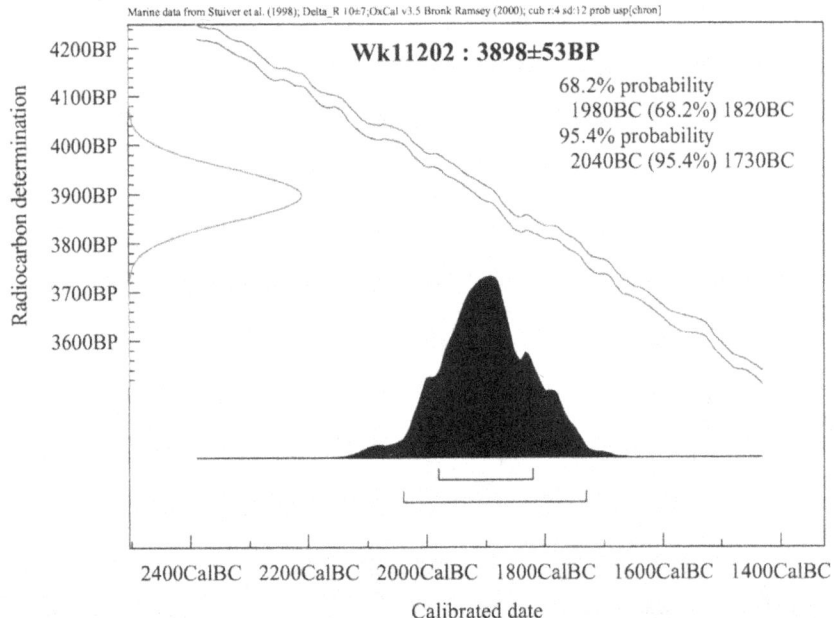

Figure 27. Radiocarbon date for the shell from Stuarts Point 1975 excavation, Cutting 2. Wendy Beck, University of New England, 2002.

10.

Winterbourne and Historical Archaeology

In 1976, I was tired of midden excavation and the endless counting of shells and decided to take Isabel McBryde's earlier advice and move on to historical sites. I had found that students became bored with shell middens and such sites provided only a limited understanding of archaeological excavation in general. During the winter of 1973, I had done a field survey of sites at Saumarez Station, near Armidale, helped by Bob Betts, who still lived there. I decided to excavate in 1976 what appeared to be the most promising of these sites, that of a small house.

My research assistant was now Mike Rowland, a New Zealander. I sent Mike Rowland to check the deposit depth and character at the potential excavation site, but he found it to be so shallow that there was, in effect, nothing to excavate.

Therefore, I had to find a more suitable site for 1976 and here Jillian Oppenheimer, of the History Department, came to my rescue in two ways. First, she directed my attention to a nineteenth-century stone ruin at Winterbourne, not far from Walcha, south of Armidale (**Figures 28–32**). Second, she offered the use of her property, *Ohio*, in Walcha, for student accommodation (**Figure 33**). It had been, I think, an orphanage, but was now disused and neglected, although not derelict.

Nevertheless, still using the May vacation for excavation presented an extra problem because the New England Tableland, where Winterbourne and 'Ohio' were situated, was much colder at that time of the year than the coast, where the midden sites excavated from 1972 to 1975 had been. Thus, Jillian Oppenheimer's help was of great importance to me. Winterbourne proved to be an interesting site, with the ruined, roofless, stone walls giving opportunities for both excavation and structural recording. Doug Hobbs was particularly good at organising the latter, which at that time necessitated time-consuming measurements and drawings.

Ohio was bitterly cold but a supply of wood offcuts from the Walcha sawmill could be burnt in the living room open fireplace and kept us warm. The students slept in the upper storey of the house, Beryl and my family in another part of the building. The previous use of the house as an orphanage had resulted in the addition of a kitchen and washing facilities to the back of the house that were of use to us during our stay but they were of wood and of poor quality and were later demolished when Jillian Oppenheimer and Bruce Mitchell got a New South Wales state heritage grant to restore the house and then decided to live in its regained comfort.

Figure 28. The remaining western part of the southern side of Winterbourne house, May 1976. Excavation of Cutting II in progress. Scale in 20-centimetre divisions.

Figure 29. Winterbourne excavation, May 1976, Cutting I completed. Scale in 20-centimetre divisions. Arrow points north.

Figure 30. Winterbourne excavation, May 1976. Excavation staff at lunchtime, near the north side of the house.

Figure 31. Mike Rowland, UNE Research Assistant, at the Winterbourne excavation, 1976.

Figure 32. The woman for whom the Winterbourne house was built: Mrs Jane Richards (wife of Captain William Richards), probably in the 1840s. Photograph in 1976 by Bill Webster, photographer at the University of New England, of an oil painting in the Walcha and District Historical Society Museum.

Figure 33. Ohio, *the front of the house in May 1976, when it housed the staff of the Winterbourne excavation. It was otherwise unoccupied at that time and in poor condition after previous use as a boy's home. It was later completely renovated by Jillian Oppenheimer and Bruce Mitchell. Its origins date from the 1840s.*

Activities in 1977 were different from previous years. Mike Rowland and I worked on the results of the Winterbourne excavation and included Jillian Oppenheimer as a historical contributor. I did not excavate that year, but Mike Rowland ran an excavation of a coastal shell midden at Sandon on the New South Wales north coast and Len Cubis, who had just completed his BA Honours degree at UNE, excavated a quarry site on Plover Island nearby. I think that it was this year that excavation ended in a disastrous storm and they had to abandon their camp for temporary motel accommodation.

The excavations might have been done in collaboration with Iain Davidson, but I am uncertain and I do not think that they were ever published. The following year, Len Cubis was killed in a car accident, as already mentioned and the botanical analysis of flotation material from the Stuarts Point excavation on which he had been working was abandoned. Mike Rowland left the UNE Department at the end of 1977 and went to a government job in Queensland.

By this time, I had also commenced a programme of archaeological aerial photography, of both prehistoric and historical sites, as mentioned above. I was flown by Frank Choate from the UNE Physics Department, who proved to be a good and careful pilot (**Figure 34**). Sometimes we took a volunteer student with us. In the 1980s, this project developed into an Australian Research Council-funded project that provided us with a more sophisticated camera and the ability to fly to remoter parts of Australia. However, the early work also produced some interesting images (**Figure 35**).

Figure 34. Frank Choate at Grafton Airport and the Cesna that he piloted, 6 August 1976. We had just flown from Armidale.

Figure 35. Indigenous bora ring and nineteenth-twentieth cemetery at Tucki Tucki, Northern New South Wales, 6 August 1976.

11.

China, Johannesburg and Nairobi

In April and May 1977, I was part of a group of 21 from Australia who made a study visit to China, organised by James Bowen, Associate Professor in the Centre for Educational Studies at the University of New England. He had led a similar study visit successfully in 1975 and it had taken him two years to arrange another one. At that time, it was very difficult to visit China and few people were able to do so.

Therefore, the previous December, I had put my name down to be included in the 1977 tour should it take place. When it happened, the tour group consisted of people from a range of occupations, not just UNE staff. The visit was three weeks long and the Chinese government was very hospitable. Mao Tse Tung had just died and Chinese politics were in an uncertain state, after surviving the rule of those referred to by the Chinese as 'The Gang of Four'.

We flew to Hong Kong for a brief cultural introduction and then went by train to Shum Chun, where we walked across a railway bridge over a river into China, passing a Chinese soldier on the way. Each of us carried our own minimal luggage, as instructed by our Australian organiser, who also told us not to wear jewellery and to generally keep a low profile.

This was a China where everyone wore blue Mao suites and men's and women's haircuts were so similar that we could not tell the difference between them at times. Travelling by air, rail and bus, depending on the distance, we visited communes, schools, hospitals, factories, archaeological sites, museums, musical performances in theatres and a memorable ballet in Beijing about the 'Small Swords' revolt in the nineteenth century. We also visited the Great Wall, the Ming Tombs in Beijing and the city of Xi'an (**Figures 36–38**).

Noticeably, we were taken to only one university. This was the Jiao Tong University in Xi'an, established in 1896 and moved to Xi'an in 1956. Its title was said to mean Tele-communication University, but its studies were apparently much broader than that. We also visited Mao's birthplace, where our group was photographed together with our interpreters and others (**Figure 39**) and we were taken to the school in Guangzhou (formerly Canton) where Mao had been a teacher early in his career.

Sadly, in spite of my request to our interpreters, we were not taken to the famous *Homo erectus* site of Choukoutien, although it is quite close to Beijing. Everything was, of course, stage-managed and pre-planned, although in one city we were allowed to walk around alone in the evening, but told to be careful not to get lost because all the street signs were in Chinese.

Figure 36. The Great Wall of China, near Beijing, is heavily curated and restored. A colour print from the 1977 tour.

Figure 37. Stone carving of an elephant, Ming Tombs, Beijing, with one of the tour group as a scale. A colour print from the 1977 visit.

Figure 38. Bronze bell from the bell tower in Xi'an, China, with James Bowen, the tour organiser, as a scale. A colour print from the 1977 visit.

Figure 39. Members of the 1977 University of New England tour of China, with interpreters and others, at Mao Tse Tung's birthplace. I am in the back row, five from the right.

I was impressed with the resourcefulness of Chinese production, despite its outdated technology at that time and impressed with the energy it displayed, even getting schoolchildren to rewire generators, for instance. I was also interested in the way that archaeology played a part in Chinese society. 'Let the past serve the present' was one of Mao Tse Tung's sayings and the museums and sites that we visited demonstrated this. As already mentioned, these included the Great Wall, the Ming Tombs in Beijing and the city of Xi'an but also we were taken to the archaeological site of Pan Pot San, near Xi'an, much of it excavated and preserved under an enormous roof.

On our return journey to Australia, we had a day or so break in Bangkok, in Thailand. However, this resulted in a serious delay. When we were about to board our flight back to Sydney, with our boarding passes already in our hands, news came through that all the air-traffic controllers in Australia had gone on strike. Many other travellers were stranded in airports around the world, but we were lucky because our boarding passes had already been issued and QANTAS was obligated to look after us. We were returned to our hotel and told that our accommodation and two meals a day would be provided but we were asked to be available at lunchtime the next day to see if the situation had changed.

However, it had not and did not change for five days while we waited for the strike to end. I had no money left and could do little to pass the time. Outside the hotel, the humidity was very high and sightseeing was out of the question. Instead, I spent several days writing an account of my impressions of China. When I got back to Australia, I sent it to *Hemisphere*, a magazine published by the Education Department of the Federal Government, that had been asking me to write something on Benin City.

By now, I had lost interest in Benin and thought that *Hemisphere* would be interested in what I had written about China. I was wrong, they declined it because they said it was 'too political'! At the time of writing this, in 2023, my 1977 paper about China remains unpublished.

I managed to phone Beryl to ask her to send me some money but at a time before the frequent use of credit cards, this took too long and I never got it. We then had difficulty getting the money back after I had returned to Australia, via Perth and a night sleeping on a bench in Sydney Airport. Altogether, the China trip was a useful one. Also, in my absence, Iain Davidson acted as departmental head.

At the end of 1976, I had been promoted to Associate Professor, but only after I had given UNE a hint by applying for a chair at the University of the Witwatersrand, in Johannesburg, South Africa. Interviewed on behalf of Witwatersrand by Mcintosh, a palaeontologist at the University of Sydney (known there as 'Black Mac'), I was then flown to Johannesburg and survived several days of interviews and of giving seminars, finishing up on a short list of two.

However, the other candidate was from the University of Cape Town and, predictably, he got the post. Nevertheless, my strategy paid off when UNE promoted me to Associate Professor. I was not sorry to escape the Witwatersrand chair. Just before my visit there, the Soweto Riots had resulted in the shooting of a number of people. Apartheid South Africa would not have suited me and I would not have been acceptable there. The rules were so restrictive that even toilets had six categories. These were for white males, white females, coloured males, coloured females, black males and black females. However, an archaeologist at the university did take me to see several of the famous early hominin caves and also some 'Iron Age' occupation sites.

Back to teaching and research at UNE, I suddenly decided that I was being too lacking in confidence about research and publication. I came to the opinion that it did not matter, I should just do it and to hell with the consequences. I had already begun to adopt this new attitude with the joint paper by myself, Emmerson and Stanley, on magnetic prospection, but it was a paper about my Saumarez fieldwork that marked the real change in my approach.

This was published in the Armidale and District Historical Proceedings. The year 1977 was not over, however and in September I flew to Nairobi to attend a Pan-African Congress meeting. During this I also worked, in my hotel, on a book about Winterbourne that was eventually published by UNE in 1978, having gone to press just before we left on study leave at the end of 1977.

12.

Study Leave in 1978

My study leave was the payback for six years of hard work at UNE. I was burnt-out from teaching and administration and wrote in my account at the time: 'It is the repetitive dullness of much of modern university work that wearies me'. The journey to Cambridge, where I wished to spend the most time, was made as interesting as possible, particularly with Beryl and the children in mind. On Wednesday, 14 December, we first flew to Sydney because for some reason the railway, on which we had intended to travel, was not operating and we were seen off from Armidale Airport by Mike Rowland and Rosemary Lucas.

In Sydney, after some Christmas shopping in the city, we got on the Indian Pacific train to Perth in Western Australia, a three-day-or-more journey. Beryl and I had a double apartment with an attached cubicle containing a shower, wash basin and toilet, Ian and Sarah had another double next to ours and Alan had a single apartment in an adjacent carriage. Everything about the train was shiny and modern and it provided good meals. It took us across New South Wales, across the Nullarbor Plain in South Australia and into Western Australia, where we arrived in Perth on Saturday, 17 December.

We then stayed in a Perth motel till Tuesday, 20 December, swimming on the City Beach on a blisteringly hot day, visiting The Western Australia Museum, the Fremantle Maritime Museum, the Perth Zoo and so on. At Fremantle, we boarded the *Kota Singapora*, a small passenger and livestock ship on which the paintwork was competing with the rust, on 20 December. That afternoon ended for me wracked by diarrhoea and vomiting but by the next morning, I had recovered enough to eat breakfast. I then spent most of the day wandering around such parts of the ship as passengers were allowed into.

This was an old vessel, built in the Netherlands in 1951 and not well looked after. Parts were dirty and smelly, the cattle and sheep contributed to this. On the stern island, the emergency steering wheel had literally fallen off onto the deck and there appeared to be no compass in the binnacle. Everywhere there was decayed woodwork, rusting steel, thickly painted over, undulating wooden decks with pitch protruding from the seams. All this indicated a ship at the end of its life but as the voyage proceeded it became apparent that the basics were sound: the engines and navigation got us to Singapore which was what really mattered and Captain Craggs, a young Australian from Fremantle, with officers and crew from a variety of countries, knew his job.

Also, the crew of the ship looked after us very well over Christmas, although they failed to persuade me to play Santa Claus. I was just not the most suitable person for the role. Each morning at sea, several dead animals were dumped over the side, they were sheep, I think. Meanwhile, we sailed north, through the Sunda Strait between Indonesia the Indonesian islands of Java and Sumatra and within sight of the volcano of Krakatoa (**Figure 40**). Near Java the sea was muddy brown in colour, from pollution that indicated the massive overpopulation there.

On 22 December, I was in a group taken up onto the bridge, where things appeared more shipshape than in some other parts of the vessel. A radar set at a range of 24 miles showed no other ships at all, our Gyro course was set at 341°. Beryl was sick with vomiting and diarrhoea but was recovering by 23 December. It took us a week to reach Singapore, after a very enjoyable voyage, including a pleasant Christmas. We arrived there on Tuesday, 27 December and stayed at a pretentious hotel in which the service was very poor and the food was usually cold (as well as very expensive).

We flew out to Dubai and London on Thursday, 29 December, after Beryl had managed to arrange a visit to the Singapore Department of Health to see how they did things. We also did a little shopping in Singapore. We landed at Gatwick Airport, in Britain, arriving there at 4.00 on the morning of Friday, 30 December and were met by Gordon, the husband of Edna, Beryl's sister and David Miller, his second son. Each had a car and they drove us to Gordon and Edna's house at Ware for breakfast.

We were then driven to Cambridge by David's wife and Gordon. David's wife took over from him as a driver after Ware because he had had so little sleep. We had not expected such kindness and it was very much appreciated. Edna had rented a two-storey house for us at 14 Beaumont Crescent, South Cambridge. It stood on a corner and we had it for a year while its owners were overseas. Alan,

Sarah and Ian went to school in Cambridge while we were there, the education authority being very helpful and kind about this.

Figure 40. Krakatoa, the volcano from the deck of the Kota Singapora, *at sea with Beryl in the foreground. December 1977.*

My purpose for the year was to write a book about my Borno research, so after family visits that we must have made in a second-hand car that we bought from another of Beryl's relatives, I flew to Nigeria as a visitor to the Nigerian Studies Centre at Ahmadu Bello University, in Zaria. I had been invited there by its Director, Ahmadu Adamu. Steve Daniels, who had moved from his teaching post at Ibadan University to a research post at Ahmadu Bello (strongly supported by a reference from me), had organised this. ABU provided me with a technical assistant, a driver and a vehicle that (I think) must have been some form of four-wheel-drive and off we went to Maiduguri for a Borno fieldtrip.

I found the Wedderburns still there and I stayed at their house as a base whenever I was in Maiduguri during my fieldwork. My intention in coming back to Borno was to improve my understanding of the region as a basis for interpreting the archaeological evidence from Daima and the other sites. My time in Australia, working with Iain Davidson, who was a product of 1960s and 1970s Cambridge whereas my background had been Cambridge in the 1950s, convinced me that I needed to know a lot more about the ethnography of Borno.

Therefore, I visited some of the archaeological sites that I knew, both south of Lake Chad (including Daima) and west of the Lake, interviewing farmers (through an interpreter) and collecting surface material (mainly pottery) from

77

various sites. Overall, I gained a better understanding of Borno and its people than I had previously. (**Figures 41–44**)

After returning to ABU, where I stayed in their guest accommodation, sitting in the dark on some nights because there was no electricity and I had only a small piece of candle, I worked for some weeks with Steve Daniels, who had remained in Zaria during my field trip. We sorted potsherds together and, in particular, took a series of close-up photographs of them for identification purposes, concentrating on their decoration. Then I went with Steve, in his car to Ibadan. The journey was very different from what it had been in the 1960s; the roads were all modern and there was no problem delay at the (railway) Jebba Bridge; it had been replaced by a new one that was for the road.

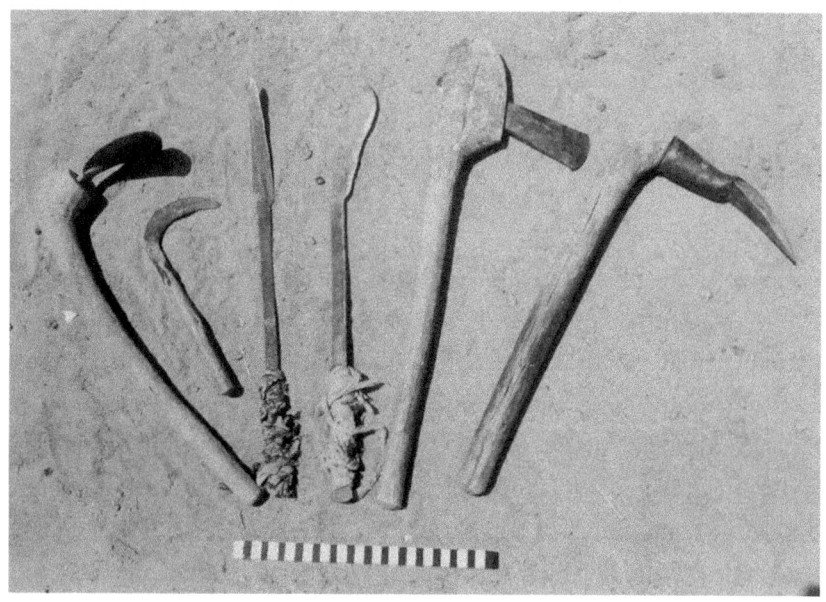

Figure 41. Farming tools used on the firki soils, Sangaya, March 1978,
Scale in centimetres.

Figure 42. A pointed stake used to make holes in the firki soil into which masakwa *seedlings were planted. March 1978.*

Figure 43. Masakwa *ready for harvest, Sangaya, Borno, March 1978. With the technical assistant provided by ABU.*

Figure 44. Masakwa *in storage-pit, Sangaya, Borno, March 1978. The pit is lined with grass and could store the grain for up to two years.*

In Ibadan, we worked on the Borno pottery stored there by me previously and we tried, without success, to float organics such as seeds out of bulk soil samples that I had saved from Daima during its excavation. The Department of Archaeology had been moved from the Institute of African Studies, where it was in the 1960s, to a new purpose-built building some distance away.

We stayed at the university house of a friend of Steve's, who lived alone, was obsessed with amateur dramatics and neglected domestic matters. We even had to buy light bulbs for the house because he had not renewed dead ones and the freezer in his fridge was so neglected that it was a solid mass of ice and unusable. Bob Soper was still at the university, living in one of its houses. Otherwise, there were very few people left who I remembered. I did see Umaru Gol briefly one morning but had no chance to speak to him and, sadly, I was never to see him again. Julius, I had already seen, I think, perhaps in Zaria.

Eventually, we drove back to Zaria, leaving Ibadan early one morning, when we saw the result of a bad road accident near the entrance to the university. A truck had overturned onto a car and my last memory of Ibadan was the widening pool of blood spreading across the road from the car occupants. Nigeria had changed but it had not really changed. Back in Zaria, I gave an evening public lecture at ABU, organised by a former Nigerian student of mine, but of course, the electricity failed and complicated things, although I continued anyway. Several days later, I flew back to Britain and returned to Cambridge.

I now had to write the book about my Borno research, but I wanted it to be different from the book about my Benin work that had been published in 1975, after many years of work. The latter had been very much in the tradition of the excavation 'report' of the 1950s and earlier. It concentrated on the archaeological evidence and provided little interpretation of that evidence.

That was how most archaeologists at the time thought that they should write. I wanted the book about Borno to present the evidence in its widest context, of environment and human history, providing a much more readable account. First, I went through all my field records and relevant published material, both of which I had been careful to bring with me to Britain. My memory is of starting to do this in Selwyn, working in Cripps Court, presumably during the Easter vacation.

In late May, however, there was a public holiday that had replaced the former Whitsun holiday and we drove to North Wales for a visit to the Lyn Peninsula, the scene of some of my earliest memories, at Llangynnadl and Borth-y-gest and we stayed near there at Chwilog (**Figure 45**). I was prepared to endure the sort of wet weather that was frequent in the area but it was sunny and warm and a very successful visit. Later in the year, we also drove to the north of Scotland and visited Orkney again. On Hoy, we found that things had changed, now there was electricity and television and I think that the yawl I had owned in the 1960s was in Stromness. Our house at Longhope had a retiled roof, although otherwise unchanged, but we stayed in a cottage at Melsetter (**Figures 46–47**).

Figure 45. Farmhouse near Chwilog, Lyn Peninsula, North Wales, where we stayed in June 1978. Ian in the doorway.

Figure 46. By 2011, my yawl in the 1960s was back at Longhope, after being owned for a while in Stromness. Said to have been built in about 1914, 'Mohican' was apparently its original name. By 2011, it had been changed from gaff rig to Bermuda rig. Photograph by Alan Connah in 2011 at Longhope.

Figure 47. Lower North Row, our house in Longhope during the 1960s, photographed by Alan Connah in 2011, with a retiled roof.

Returning to the Borno book, I moved to work in a small 'study' upstairs at our Beaumont Crescent house but also spent a lot of time at the University Library searching for material. I used the UL more in 1978 than I had in the 1950s, but it was still moderately quiet, not overcrowded as it was to become in later years as Cambridge postgraduate students increased in number. I also worked in the Department of Archaeology and Anthropology library and other Cambridge libraries.

In addition, I located and photographed Borno material in the British Museum store and at the Horniman Museum in London and Beryl found information for me in the Rhodes House archives at Oxford. After the passage of years, it is impossible to remember just what was done and when, but then I had a stroke of luck.

I attended some sort of party where I met Robin Derricourt who was at that time the archaeological editor in Cambridge for Cambridge University Press. When I told him about my planned book, he suggested I should submit a proposal to CUP, so I did this and it was eventually accepted and I signed a contract for the book. I had decided to call it *Four Thousand Years in Africa* and Derricourt was amused when I changed the title to *Three Thousand Years in Africa* in the interests of modesty and the avoidance of exaggeration. However, I failed to ensure that the subtitle reflected current changing attitudes when I included in it the phrase 'man and environment', rather than 'people and environment'; an oversight that I regret.

I worked hard on the Borno book and I tried to make it tell a story that would be interesting for readers as well as important. As the title suggested, the book indicated that Africa did have a past and that it was a past that mattered. As the months went by, I also wrote a paper about Australian aerial photography for *Antiquity,* an interim report for *Nyame Akuma* on my recent work in Nigeria and a report on a magnetic survey at Forster, New South Wales, that I had done with John Stanley from UNE in 1977.

In addition, in 1978 the Winterbourne book was published as mentioned above and I wrote a paper for a festschrift for Raymond Mauny, that was not published till 1981. I declined an invitation to contribute to a big book on archaeology, the details of which I have forgotten because I just did not have the time. Altogether, it was a most productive year and near its end, when Iain Davidson on vacation in Britain found me working in the UL, I had virtually finished. Nevertheless, there were still things to do, particularly with the illustrations, to which Doug Hobbs was to contribute so brilliantly in the months that followed.

In 1978, I also gave an invited paper to the Archaeology Society in the university department and talked to many members of the university, both staff and students. Subsequently, I was to regard the Borno book as the best thing that I ever wrote (**Figure 48**).

New Studies in Archaeology

Three thousand years in Africa

Man and his environment in the Lake Chad region of Nigeria

GRAHAM CONNAH

Figure 48. The book about the Borno research, written in 1978 after many years of delay.

13.

Excavations at Bagots Mill and Reddestone Creek

I returned to UNE early in 1979, to find that I had more than enough work to do for the Borno book. Doug Hobbs, who I had appointed as a departmental technician, was hard at work on the illustrations for the book. At that time his work was mainly hand-drawn but by the mid-1980s he was doing it by computer. We worked well together. I would sketch out what I needed, which he would scan into the computer as a basis for the drawing that he then produced. Later in 1979, I invited John Mulvaney to visit the department and while he was in Armidale, I took him to see the site of Bagots Mill, which I intended to excavate. He clearly approved of the idea and towards the end of the year, I ran the first of three excavations there (**Figures 49–53**).

Figure 49. John Mulvaney, 1925–2016, late in life. He was a remarkable personality: a real 'dinky di' Australian.

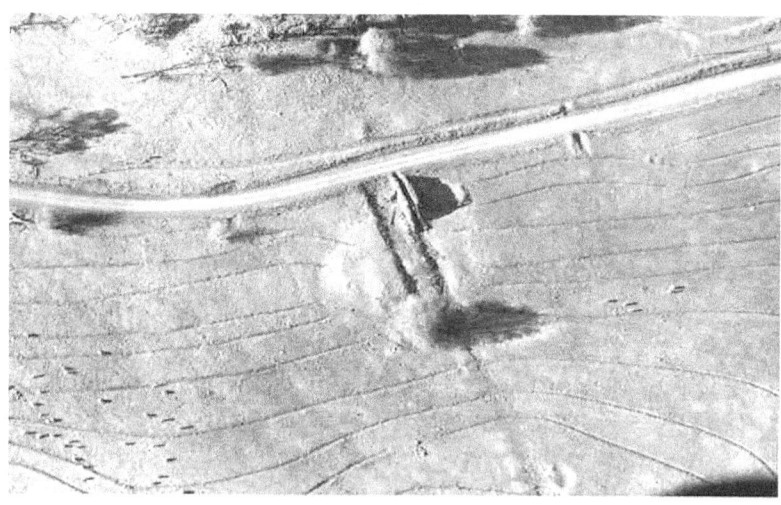

Figure 50. Aerial photograph of the Bagots Mill site in July 1977, before excavation. View approximately from the north-east.

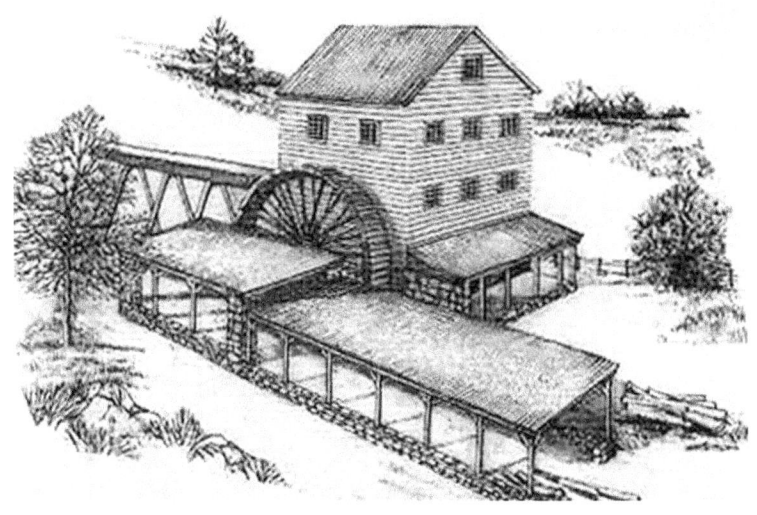

Figure 51. Bagots Mill, as Christopher Thomas Bagot might have intended, but it was never completed. Drawing by Elizabeth Dixon.

Figure 52. Bagots Mill, inside of wheel-chamber, completely excavated, looking towards the inlet end, 1980. Scale in centimetres.

Figure 53. Bagots Mill, Alan Connah on top of the wheel-chamber south-west wall with its axle bearing-block of granite. Probably 1980.

Earlier that year I had managed to appoint New Zealander Mike Morwood to a lectureship. In 1980, megafauna bones were reported from a sapphire mine near Glen Innes, at a place called Reddestone Creek. I ran an excavation there in the July.

It was mid-winter when I tackled the site; we worked some two metres below water level pumping almost continually and the pump was frozen up every morning. We had to dig a sump for the water pumped from the cutting before we could commence work. The participating students and I lived in an extremely

90

cold, unheated, disused house in the area. After several weeks, I moved out to a rented caravan in Glen Innes.

David Horton, a palaeontologist, and I collaborated and jointly published an account of the excavation, which we did quite quickly, but the additional detailed study of the fauna (that was mostly *Diprotodon*) was never completed to my knowledge. Our basic research question was whether there was an association between human activity and the bones and we found that was definitely not the case (**Figures 54–56**).

Figure 54. The Reddestone Creek excavation completed, July 1980. Sampling in progress for pollen at the bottom left. Scale in centimetres.

Figure 55. Reconstruction of a Diprotodon. *Most bones found at Reddestone Creek were of this extinct animal that was up to 4 metres long.*

Figure 56. Bill Cameron, local historian of Glen Innes, who helped with liaison for Reddestone Creek, Bagots Mill and other places. Northern Magazine 13 October 1985: 2. *The University of New England awarded him an honorary degree in recognition of his contributions.*

A legacy of the excavation at Reddestone Creek was the beginning of a very painful back that I damaged while trying to fill in the cutting with the very heavy clay that had been removed. Overall, it was a difficult time and I had to pay Luke Godwin, then one of our postgraduate students, to complete the backfilling of the excavation because I was temporally crippled. Nevertheless, I have a memory that later, in 1980, I ran a second excavation at Bagots Mill.

14.
Research Below Ground and From the Air

In March 1979, road works on Mount Beef, near Uralla, south of Armidale, revealed a small hole that enabled me to enter a gold-mining tunnel that probably dated from 1852 to c.1880 (**Figures 57–59**). It had been cut into decomposed, unstable white granite, presumably probing for a deep lead beneath the basalt hilltop and apparently had been abandoned when the granite dipped too steeply and made the removal of material from the tunnel too difficult. It was an opportunistic venture that failed, as so many other mining ventures have done, although it reached at least 74 metres into the hill before it was abandoned.

Figure 57. Me in the Mount Beef gold-mining tunnel, Uralla, March 1979. The light in the distance is the entrance. The tunnel was approximately 1.75 metres wide and 1.70 metres high. Photograph by Shirley Dawson, UNE Photography Department.

Figure 58. Me in the Mount Beef gold-mining tunnel, Uralla, March 1979. A fall at c.67 metres from the entrance is an example of the dangers of nineteenth-century mining. Photograph by Shirley Dawson, UNE Photography Department.

Figure 59. The Mount Beef gold-mining tunnel, Uralla, March 1979. Pick-marks on the walls of the tunnel, cut by hand. Scale in centimetres. Photograph by Shirley Dawson, UNE Photograph Department.

During the first half of the 1980s Alan Jones and I did a lot of aerial photography, funded by our Australian Research Council grant, which enabled us to purchase a Hasselblad camera and special lenses. It also made it possible to fly to more distant locations in Queensland, far western New South Wales and the Victorian border. Work in the far north included a visit to Mornington Island in the Gulf of Carpentaria and we took some impressive photographs of the adjacent coast. One of these won the second prize in a UNE photographic competition. We also photographed historical sites in New England and on the north coast of New South Wales (**Figures 60–63**).

Flying in a New South Wales National Parks and Wildlife Service Cessna, I was later able to get permission to remove the door from the plane and photograph directly not through the window. This was an interesting experience, especially when the plane banked to that side and when we were taking off or landing. My seatbelt needed to be securely fastened! The Cessna had high wings which made it possible to get a clear view when photographing.

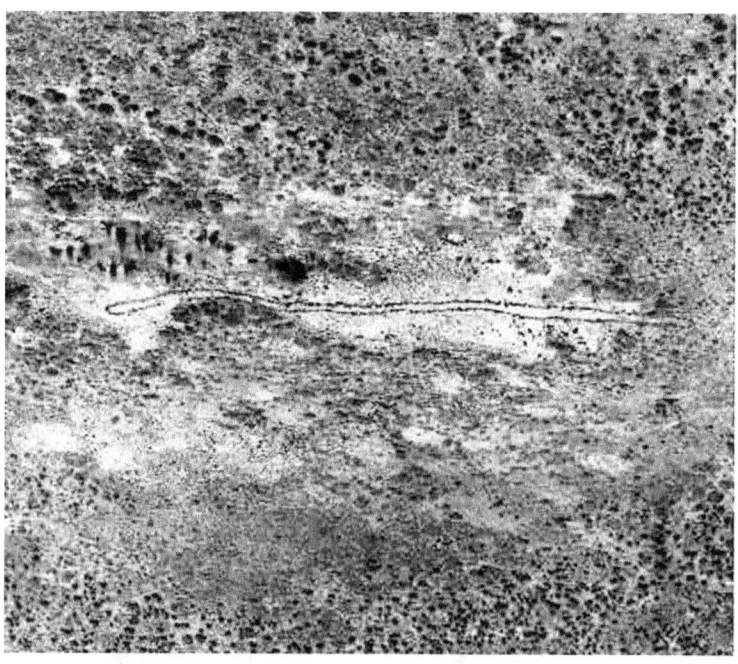

Figure 60. Aerial photograph of indigenous track, Pindera Downs near Tibooburra, far western New South Wales. November 1980.

Figure 61. Aerial photograph of indigenous fish-traps on the coast of Bayley Island, north Queensland. May 1982.

Figure 62. Aerial photograph of Gostwyk woolshed, near Armidale NSW An unusual octagonal structure built of wood in 1851. The other buildings and the yards are of later date. September 1980.

Figure 63. Aerial photograph of Trial Bay Gaol, 1886–1919, north coast of New South Wales. January 1982.

In 1985, I managed to arrange for the annual conference of the Australian Society for Historical Archaeology to be held in Armidale, at the University of New England. This was successful but inevitably it was difficult to attract as many participants as could be done for conferences in Sydney, Melbourne or other major cities.

15.

Back to Nigeria

The year 1981 started differently because I made my last visit to Nigeria. Again, I was invited there by Mahdi Adamu, the Director of the Nigerian Studies Centre at Ahmadu Bello University, in Zaria. I arrived in Kano by air from London on Monday 12 January at 4.30 am. Steve Daniels had left Nigeria by then but the Centre provided me with a graduate assistant called Joe Jemkur, a vehicle (a large Volkswagen bus with double wheels on each side at the back), a driver called Ahmadu Bello and a technician called Mathias Opuana (**Figure 64**).

I intended to spend time in the field in Borno but also back at the University analysing the evidence that we recovered during the fieldwork. My hope was to find evidence of an occupation that predated Daima and the other Borno sites that I had worked on previously. I reasoned that if I searched further south, near the base of the Mandara Mountains, I would be able to find a landscape that had emerged from a shrinking early Holocene Lake Chad before the northern part of the clay plains emerged.

After I had slept for the rest of Monday, we got everything ready on Tuesday in order to leave on Wednesday, 14 January. This we were able to do because the team I was to work with had done everything possible in preparation. It was an impressive performance by them, for which I was extremely grateful. Before leaving Zaria, I met Dr F.R. Effah-Gyemfi, who was then teaching archaeology at Ahmadu Bello University.

Having left Zaria at 11.00 am, later than intended because of delays, we arrived at the Wedderburns' house in Maiduguri at 10.30 pm. There I met Steve Pern, who was staying with them recovering from infective hepatitis which he got while attempting to walk from Lake Chad to Cameroun with pack donkeys. This seemed pointless to me but it seems that he travelled around Lake Turkana a little while ago and wrote quite a good popular book about his experiences. He intended a similar book on his Nigerian trip but had to call it off and return to Britain. He planned to come back to Nigeria later in the year and finish his journey.

On arrival in Maiduguri, I found the Wedderburns as friendly as ever and I stayed with them at times during my Borno trip. It was the last occasion that I saw them because they then went briefly, I think to Tanzania and after that retired to Britain. However, things had changed in Maiduguri by 1981 and Nan Wedderburn had made the best of them. She got me an interview with the local television station and arranged for me to give a public lecture at the university that existed by then in Maiduguri. Clearly, she had made an impact on the development of the Borno State, having written a schoolbook in Kanuri.

On Thursday, 15 January, we looked for, but could not find, a cultural officer of the Borno State Government with whom Nan Wedderburn had arranged for me to get the appropriate clearances and assistance while in Borno. In the late afternoon, with Jemkur and Mathias, I called on the Member of the House of Assembly for Gwoza at his house. His name was Peter Zadra and Gwoza was my preferred base for the intended fieldwork. I got his support and he gave me the names of local contacts if we needed help.

On Friday, 16 January, with Nan Wedderburn, we looked for the cultural officer of the State Government again and found him. He took us to the Commissioner for Home Affairs, Information and Culture, where I did an impromptu speech about what we were hoping to do in Borno that was videoed for local television, as Nan Wedderburn had arranged. We then visited the Permanent Secretary for Home Affairs and the Acting Deputy Director of the Borno State Arts Council. Although it was now midday with Friday prayers looming, we got our letter of authority and arranged to meet a representative of the Arts Council, Alhaji Grema, the next morning to go on a fact-finding run to arrange accommodation and look the study area over.

This we did on Saturday, 17 January, going to Gwoza to see the local government people who, amazingly, had already received the letter of authority written only the day before. They promised to find us accommodation in Gwoza if we came on Tuesday with our loads, Monday being the Prophet's Birthday and therefore a holiday. We had a look at the intended study area and found that it was bounded by Ngurosoye, Dar-el-Jimeil, Pulka and Kirawa, being situated between the Bama-to-Gwoza road to the west, the Cameroun border to the east, the Bama Ridge to the north and the Gwoza Hills, near the Mandara Mountains, to the south. We decided to record 'Collection Points' rather than 'sites' and looked at and listed the first five. Then we returned to Maiduguri.

On Sunday 18 February, I spent the day dealing with an 18x15-centimetre pot containing a total of 622 carnelian and quartz beads that had been found at Ala, near Dikwa, during the 1980 wet season and given to Nan Wedderburn. This was at the Wedderburns' house. I reconstructed the pot on Sunday and Monday and published it and the beads some years later, in 2001. I visited Ala, with the Wedderburns, and photographed it and the beads at that time. In the evening of 19 January, I had dinner at Ekhart Wulf's house, a German linguist interested in the Mandara area, who was working at the University of Maiduguri.

Also, there was Judy Butterman, a lecturer in history at the University of Maiduguri. Ekhart Wulf told me that the languages of my intended study area, in rough order of importance, were Kanuri, Shuwa, Gamergu, Mandara, Glavda. Hausa was very little spoken. I left Maiduguri on Tuesday, 20 January and travelled to Bama. There I saw Ibrahim Abba, Secretary to the Local Government at Bama, Abba Sanda, Secretary of the Emirate Council at Bama and the Emir. Then I went on to Gwoza and got accommodation in the Local Government Rest House. A house built by the contractors Cubitts that had been promised for my use became available later.

On Wednesday, 21 January, at last, we started the fieldwork, with a local headmaster, Mohammed Alamin Bello, provided by the Local Government at Bama. During the fieldwork, we looked at a total of 41 Collection Points, aided by local informants in some cases. However, based on my team in Gwoza, I was only able to find more mound sites like those to the north. We excavated one of these at Gagava Nyandera Amtha (Collection Point 37), a mound close to the Mandara Mountains but were only able to spend a couple of days on it and had to backfill and abandon it before we had reached a convincing 'Natural'. It was later radiocarbon dated to about the same time as the mounds to the north (**Figure 65–66**).

A decade later, a German research team showed that smaller mounds situated on estuarine deposits at the margins of the early Holocene Lake Chad were the earlier sites that I had been seeking. In 1981, I lacked the detailed geomorphological information on the area that was needed to discover them but I think that some of the low mounds and sherds that we found were an indication that we might have been seeing evidence of the earlier Gajiganna Culture or its predecessor, later studied by the Germans.

While at Gwoza, we climbed to the top of the nearest part of the Mandara Mountains on Sunday, 31 January and visited the village of Guduf Babaya-Gawa at the top. We recorded several sites there, including a large rock shelter that seemed to have only a limited floor deposit and was known by the villagers as 'Buhe's House'. We also saw some evidence of local ironworking that was probably of late date and I collected a sample of magnetite, a black iron ore of high purity.

In addition, we were shown an impressive bored stone, sub-rectangular in shape, measuring 21x19 centimetres and 13.7 centimetres thick, that had an hourglass perforation of 6.5–3.3 centimetres diameter. The villagers called this 'Buhe's Bead' and it was most likely a digging-stick weight of an unknown date. It took us all day to climb up the mountain and descend afterwards, but the outcome was a little disappointing from the archaeological point of view. It was also very tiring.

While in Borno, I gave a lecture at the History Department of the University of Maiduguri that was well received, I think that I also gave a lecture at the University of Zaria before leaving Nigeria. Overall, it had been a successful trip but too much time had been spent on official matters that had to be attended to. The only solution would have been to make the time spent in Nigeria longer and that was just not possible because of my work at the University of New England.

Figure 64. The Borno fieldwork team, 1981. Left to right: Ahmadu Bello, Mathias Opuana, me, Joe Jemkur.

Figure 65. Excavating at Gagava Nawayanda Amthe, 1981.
A test excavation that had to be done quickly.

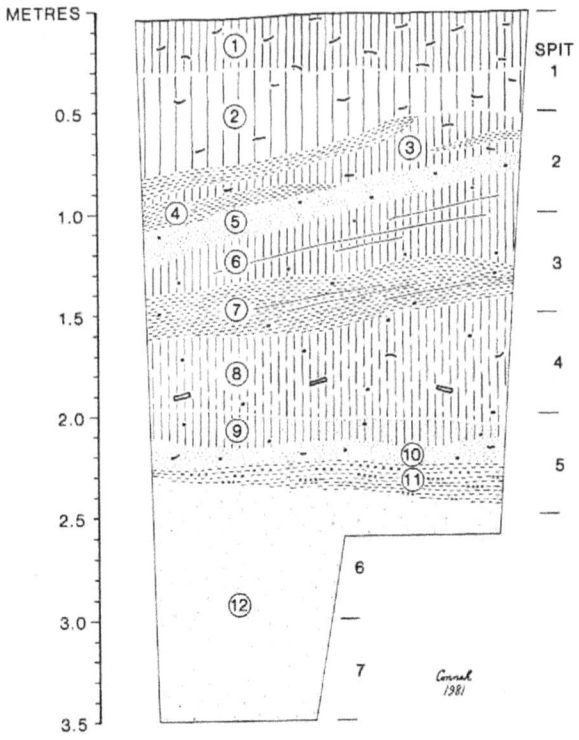

Figure 66. The east section of Gagava Nawayanda Amthe excavation, 1981.
East section of test excavation at Gagava Nawayanda Amthe (B119). 1: Brown/grey sand and gravel with sherds (cultivated soil). 2: Grey sand and gravel, with sherds. 3: Brown/grey sand and gravel, fewer sherds. 4: Pale grey lenses. 5: Black/brown earth, flecked with charcoal. 6: Brown/grey sand and gravel, flecked with charcoal, some fine banding. 7: Pale grey sand and fine gravel, flecked with charcoal, some fine banding. 8: Brown/grey sand and gravel, flecked with charcoal, sherds and bones; jumbled material. 9: Brown sand and gravel, flecked with charcoal. 10: Black/brown earth, flecked with charcoal and sherds. 11: Pale grey ashy sand and fine gravel. 12: Light brown sandy fine gravel, probably merging into Natural below limits of excavation.

Following the Borno work, I wrote an account of it for private distribution, published an interim report with Joe Jemkur in *Nyame Akuma and* published a comprehensive paper in *The African Archaeological Review*. However, much of 1981 was taken up with the publication of *Three Thousand Years* and the preparation of my Australian fieldwork methods book for publication, although it did not appear until 1983.

Time was also spent on other writing, including the Reddestone Creek paper and on founding *The Australian Journal of Historical Archaeology*, the first issue of which appeared in 1983. It was also in 1981 that I managed to appoint Peter Brown to a lectureship in palaeoanthropology (previously known as physical anthropology). Bagots Mill had to wait until 1982 for its third and final excavation.

16.

More Study Leave, Regentville and Recognition

At the end of 1982, I went on study leave for 1983. This was sooner than I should have been able to go but I had help from a member of the UNE administrative staff who knew how to bend the rules and did so in my favour, perhaps because he had worked in West Africa at some time. Again, I went to Cambridge, where David Phillipson had arranged for me to be a visiting fellow at the African Studies Centre in Free School Lane, of which the director was then my old Nigerian acquaintance A.T. (Dick) Grove of Downing College.

During the year, I was able to write most of the first edition of my book *African Civilizations* and I published twice on Australian aerial archaeology, both times in collaboration with Alan Jones of the UNE Geography Department. Again, Edna Miller, Beryl's sister, had found us good accommodation, this time in an apartment in the south of Cambridge, although I cannot remember the address. Alan was in his first year at university, so he stayed in Australia, but Sarah and Ian went to school in Cambridge.

During the year I gave, I think, four lectures in the Department of Archaeology and Anthropology at the request of David Phillipson and participated in numerous university activities. The most memorable of these was a presentation at St John's College by John Alexander, on the Egyptian site of Qasr Ibrim, of which he was the director. I was so impressed by the organics preserved on this dry site that I was determined to become involved with it. I had long wished to escape the limitations of the poor preservation of archaeological evidence and here was a chance to do so.

In addition, I thought that Egypt could only be understood in the context of Africa as a whole and that to understand Africa, it was essential to know about Egypt. However, our finances were tight in 1983, partly because Australia had devalued the Australian dollar. To help, Beryl was working in aged care in Cambridge.

Nevertheless, I decided to visit the site during the coming excavation season, which occurred in alternate years. I needed a couple of weeks to assess the situation and gather evidence to use in an application to the Australian Research Grants Council for funds. John Alexander could cover the costs of my visit while I was there, but I had to get myself there. Without me asking, Nora McMillan generously gave me £600 to fly to Egypt and I did so at the end of December. I was briefly in Cairo and then went by air to Aswan, where I joined the excavation team that seemed to be mainly volunteers, not professionals.

I was briefly in a hotel at Aswan, during which time I hired a feluka and its two-man crew, to have a sail on the Nile. Then all of us boarded the *Gerf Hussein,* a houseboat left over from the 1960s United Nations rescue project caused by the construction of the Aswan High Dam. The vessel was in a poor state and its engines no longer worked, so that it had to be towed by a tug together with a barge carrying the Egyptian labour force. It took five days to reach Qasr Ibrim because Lake Nasser is so large, the boat had to tie up each night and we stopped to visit several archaeological sites on the way.

At Qasr Ibrim, I found a landscape that was like a battlefield in World War I, unfilled holes everywhere and other spaces occupied by spoil dumps, a scene of utter desolation. Excavation had gone on there for years under different directors, one of whom had been Martin Plumley, a fellow of Selwyn College who I regarded as more of a historian and linguist than an archaeologist. I spent approximately a week at Qasr Ibrim, looking at the site and at the activities of the different members of the excavation team. Pottery, botanical evidence, animal bones, basketry, textiles and other materials were being examined by individual specialists.

I made a careful written record of what I saw and took many photographs for use in my intended Australian Research Grants Council application for funds. My plan was to be able to participate in the next season, that would be in 1986 and for that, I would need substantial finance. At the end of my time at the site, I travelled on the tug to Abu Simbel, from where I flew back to Cairo and subsequently to Britain. I realised that I would have to learn some Arabic to be able to communicate with the labour force, who were apparently from Quft in southern Egypt each season. I also had the task of working with The Egypt

Exploration Society in London, which held the excavation licence from the Egyptian government.

Looking back on it, I was too optimistic, most Egyptian archaeology was old-fashioned and the work at Qasr Ibrim was not much better, in spite of John Alexander's genuine efforts to improve things. I was going to have a difficult task trying to do something different.

During 1984, I wrote several book reviews but spent much of my time preparing and editing a second volume of *The Australian Journal of Historical Archaeology*. I also applied to the Australian Research Grants Council of the Federal Government for funds for my intended work at Qasr Ibrim but the application was unsuccessful. However, I submitted a revised application in 1985 that did succeed.

In addition, in 1985 I wrote a paper on agricultural intensification and sedentism in the firki of N.E. Nigeria, for a book edited by Ian Farrington called *Prehistoric intensive agriculture in the tropics*, which was published by BAR as International Series 232. Another major activity during 1985 was an excavation at Regentville, near Penrith. I undertook this in collaboration with Sydney University, in an attempt to combine our resources and students. It proved to be a disappointing venture. However, in 1986, I published a paper in the ASHA Journal with my account of the excavation (**Figure 67**).

Figure 67. Excavating part of the site of Sir John Jamison's house at Regentville, near Penrith, New South Wales, 1985. Scale in 50-centimetre divisions.

Figure 68. The UNE Chancellor, Robert Robertson Cunningham and me at the presentation of D.Litt. April 1984.

Figure 69. Beryl at her BA graduation ceremony, University of New England, 20 April 1985.

Figure 70. Alan, Beryl and me at Beryl's graduation ceremony, University of New England, 20 April 1985.

In 1984, I received a Doctor of Letters (D.Litt.) from the University of New England for the Benin book and the Borno book, which had been assessed by external examiners. This was the highest degree that could be awarded and solved the problem of my lack of a PhD because it was a superior degree to that. The following year, Beryl received her BA degree at the university (**Figures 68–70**).

Nine years as an Associate Professor ended for me in 1985 because the university at last decided to create a chair in archaeology. Ron Lampert, an Australian prehistoric archaeologist, was put on the shortlist along with me. Known to be critical of UNE inertia and wanting change, I expected prejudice would result in my failure to get the appointment, but I was wrong.

While I waited to be interviewed by the selection committee, one of its members, a professor from some other part of the university than the Arts Faculty, whose name I have forgotten, came out and gave me some kind advice. Essentially, he warned me to be careful about what I said so as not to antagonise the committee. I was most grateful to him for this advice, which I followed and I was offered the chair, which I subsequently accepted. In 1985 and 1986, I edited and published two more issues of the ASHA Journal and in 1987 UNE published my inaugural lecture that I had given in October 1986, with the title 'The purposes of archaeology'.

17.
Qasr Ibrim and Historical Archaeology Writing

December 1985 saw me back in Egypt to participate in the 1986 Qasr Ibrim excavation season. After brief stops in Cairo and Aswan, I went to the site by boat on Lake Nasser, as in 1983. I think that it was this year that the propeller fell off the tug and had to be reattached during the journey. It was typical of the poor organisation. John Alexander gave me a partly excavated house site to complete, which I tackled by my own methods, not the mostly crude ones used at the site. I had a dozen workmen who I had to teach how to use trowels and brushes rather than hoes and I had difficulties giving instructions in Arabic because none of them spoke English.

I had to be out of bed at 5 am each day and, after a cup of tea, I was on the site by 6 am as the sun rose. Breakfast was at 9.30 and we then worked until 1.30 pm, when we had lunch. The afternoons were spent on the boat by most of the others, working on analysis, but I returned to my excavation to work on my records. We met for drinks in the evenings, followed by dinner. On my site, I had to remove most of a large spoil dump to give me enough access to the site. Nevertheless, I was able to do a very careful piece of excavation in a site of considerable stratigraphic complexity that had maximum preservation of wood and other organics (**Figures 71–81**).

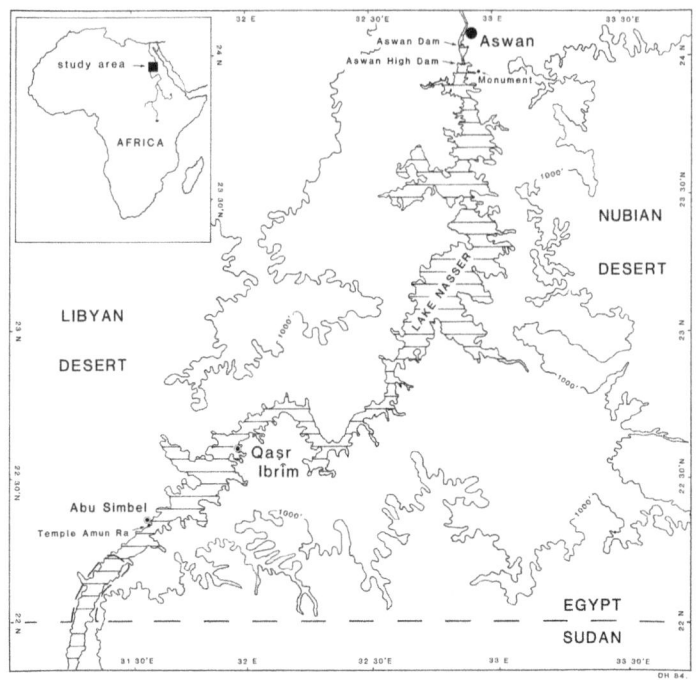

Figure 71. Southern Egypt with the location of Qasr Ibrim in relation to Lake Nasser and the surrounding deserts. Drawn by Douglas Hobbs.

Figure 72. The Gerf Hussein moored at Qasr Ibrim during the 1985–1986 excavation. Photograph by Graham Connah.

Figure 73. The workroom on the Gerf Hussein in 1985–1986, Left Peter French, Right John Alexander. Photograph by Graham Connah.

Figure 74. Three of my workmen at Qasr Ibrim in 1985–1986. Their clothes indicate that it was a Friday. Photograph by Graham Connah.

Figure 75. Me working on records at the Qasr Ibrim excavation, 1986. Photograph by Tony Bonner.

Figure 76. North-west part of the completed excavation of House 1037 at Qasr Ibrim, Egypt, 1986.

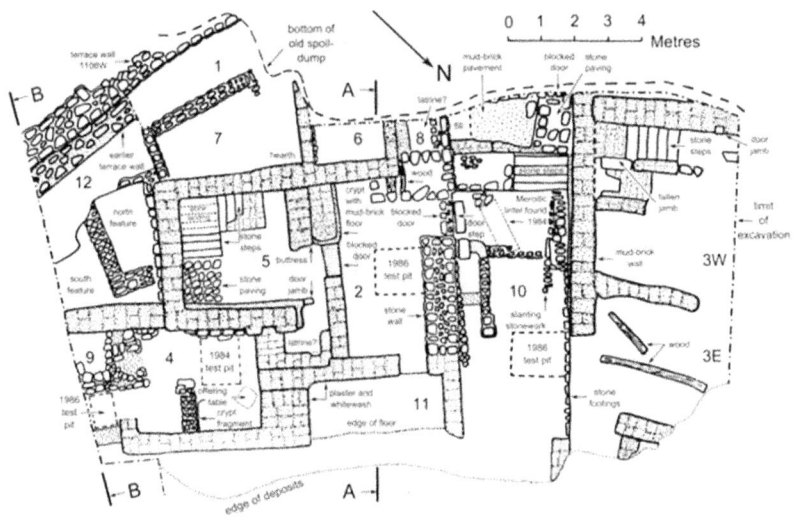

Figure 77. Plan of the completed excavation of House 1037 at Qasr Ibrim, Egypt, 1986.

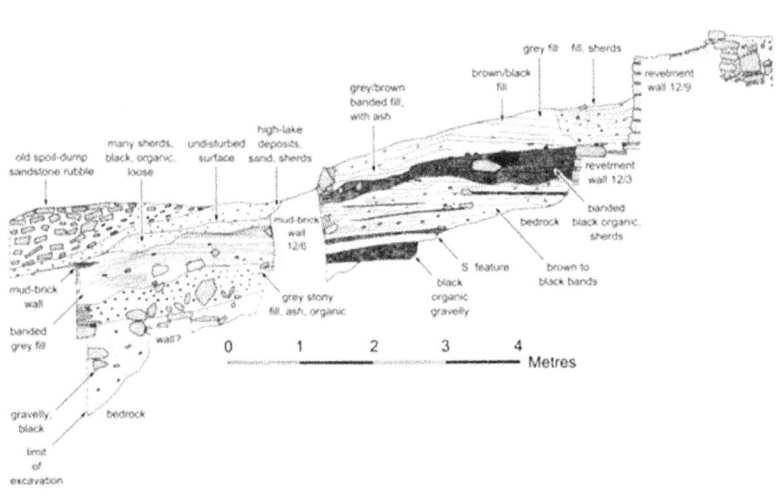

Figure 78. Sections were absent or rare in earlier excavations at Qasr Ibrim but this is 1986 Section B-B (See Figure 77).

Figure 79. Wooden figure from the 1986 Qasr Ibrim excavation, an example of organic preservation. Scale in centimetres.

Figure 80. Rope preserved in the Qasr Ibrim deposits, excavated in 1986. Scale in centimetres.

Figure 81. In my study at the University of New England, 1986, after the Qasr Ibrim excavation.

Pottery was abundant on the site and other finds included wood, baskets like the modern ones used to remove our spoil, other organics and metal. I started work at the site just before Christmas, that we celebrated on the boat. Meanwhile, John Alexander was *emptying* tombs and houses and Boyce Driscoll, an American, was *digging up* a temple. Their work seemed obsessed with plans and artefacts rather than the stratigraphy, which was my focus. I did get support, however, from Pam Rose and Peter Rowly-Conwy, both with a Cambridge background, who clearly appreciated what I was trying to do.

I found the attitude of some others of the excavation staff less understanding and the Rais, as the foreman of the workmen was called, was most uncooperative. I did the best job I could do in the circumstances and amassed copious notes, section-drawings (not usually drawn at Qasr Ibrim!) and photographs, as well as collecting samples for radiocarbon dating. Each day was very hot as Qasr Ibrim is in a part of Nubia where it almost never rains, so there was one day when work had to stop because of a dust storm. Walking back to the boat one lunchtime, I came face to face with a hyena but I turned and walked away, the animal doing the same I think and later I heard some of the workmen throwing stones at it.

It was to be 2016 by the time I got around to publishing an account of my 1986 excavation at Qasr Ibrim, which I did in collaboration with David Pearson. So much for branching out in a new direction! I had not adequately appreciated that Egyptology was dominant and archaeology got less attention. As for John Alexander, he had been unwell at the end of the 1986 season and afterwards, he gave up directing the site. Work there continued for two more seasons with a field survey of the site surrounds by Pamela Rose and an excavation by Mark Horton, both of which were later published. The level of Lake Nasser subsequently rose so high that apparently the site was gradually submerged.

I worked hard in 1987. The first edition of *African Civilizations* was published and I edited another issue of the ASHA Journal. The main task, however, was the writing of a book on Australian historical archaeology that Cambridge University Press asked me to do for publication in the Australian Bicentennial Year of 1988. I was asked to do this by Robin Derricourt, who was now running a Cambridge University Press office in Sydney.

I had just several months to write the book. To do it in such a short time I had to be out of bed each morning by 5 am, to be able to do three hours of work on it, have breakfast and then go to UNE at 9 am to do a day's work there. It was the only way that I could do it in the available time because it involved a lot of reading, correspondence with other archaeologists and careful thinking. I called it *Of the Hut I builded*, making use of a quotation from a Henry Lawson poem, although, in a later edition, this was changed to *The Archaeology of Australia's History* at the request of Cambridge University Press. The new title had been the subtitle in the first edition. (**Figure 82–84**).

The ARCHAEOLOGY

of Australia's History

Graham CONNAH

Figure 82. The 1993 edition of the 1988 book about Australian historical archaeology, with a more suitable title.

Figure 83. One of the illustrations in The Archaeology of Australia's History. *St Nicholas's Anglican Church, Saumarez Ponds, near Armidale, NSW. Constructed in 1864, this is one of the few surviving structures from a former rural settlement. Photograph by Lionel Gilbert.*

Figure 84. The archaeology of war. An illustration in The Archaeology of Australia's History. *This is the only surviving example of a German World War I tank anywhere in the world and was captured by the Australian Army. It had a crew of 18 to 23 men. Photograph by Carlos Picasso, courtesy of the Queensland Museum.*

18.

Saumarez Excavations and Structural Analysis

During the 1980s, I ran a training excavation for my students at Saumarez Old Homestead, near Armidale and therefore conveniently near the university. It continued over five short periods from 1987 to 1999. To make it possible to work in the uncertain weather of the colder times of the year when the excavations had to be done (to suit the University's timetable), I got the UNE Maintenance Department to make a steel, plastic and wooden cover for the central part of the site (**Figure 85**).

This was inspired by similar protection that I had seen in Canada in 1981. It had to be repaired on one occasion but was a great improvement on the archaeological site conditions that I had known over the years, when in Britain, for instance, one usually just got wet or bitterly cold. In between the excavation periods, I had the excavated surface covered with black plastic to discourage weed growth. As should be the case even for training excavations, I eventually published the project in 2019.

Figure 85. Saumarez Old Homestead excavation, 1985. This was a training site for UNE students, with protection from the weather.

Another part of field training for students consisted of work on the archaeology of standing structures, undertaking the structural analysis of buildings at Saumarez Station and at the properties of Newholme, a little to the north of Armidale and Abington, on the western slopes of the tableland near Bundarra (**Figures 86–90**). This was later published in 2021: as *The archaeology and architecture of farm buildings at Saumarez Station, Armidale, New South Wales*.

Figure 86. The store at Saumarez Station from the south-west.

Figure 87. The granary at Abington, recorded as built in 1863. In March 1993.

Figure 88. The woolshed at Newholme from its west end, a recycled building.
April 1989.

Newholme also provided a challenge for students in the form of the collapsed remains of a wooden sawmill (**Figures 89 and 90**).

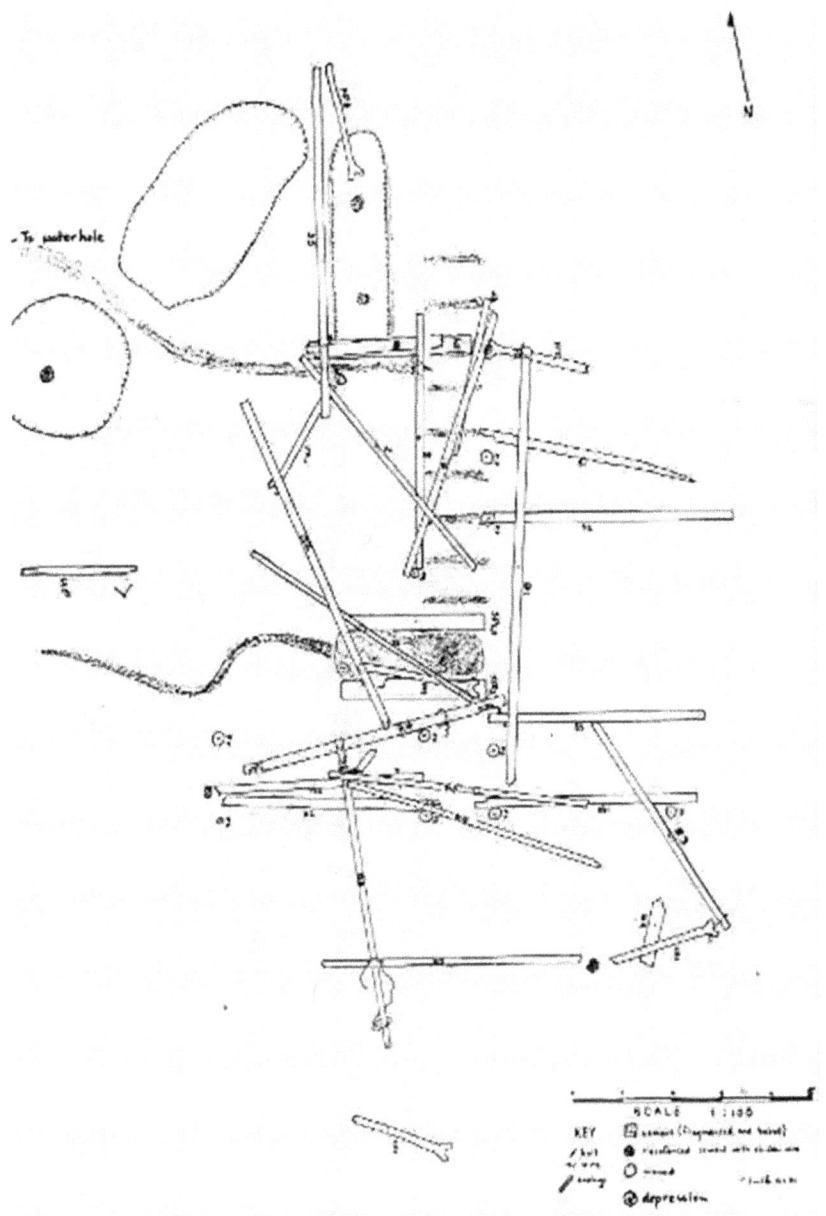

Figure 89. The Newholme sawmill site as found in 1989. Drawn by Carol Lentfer.

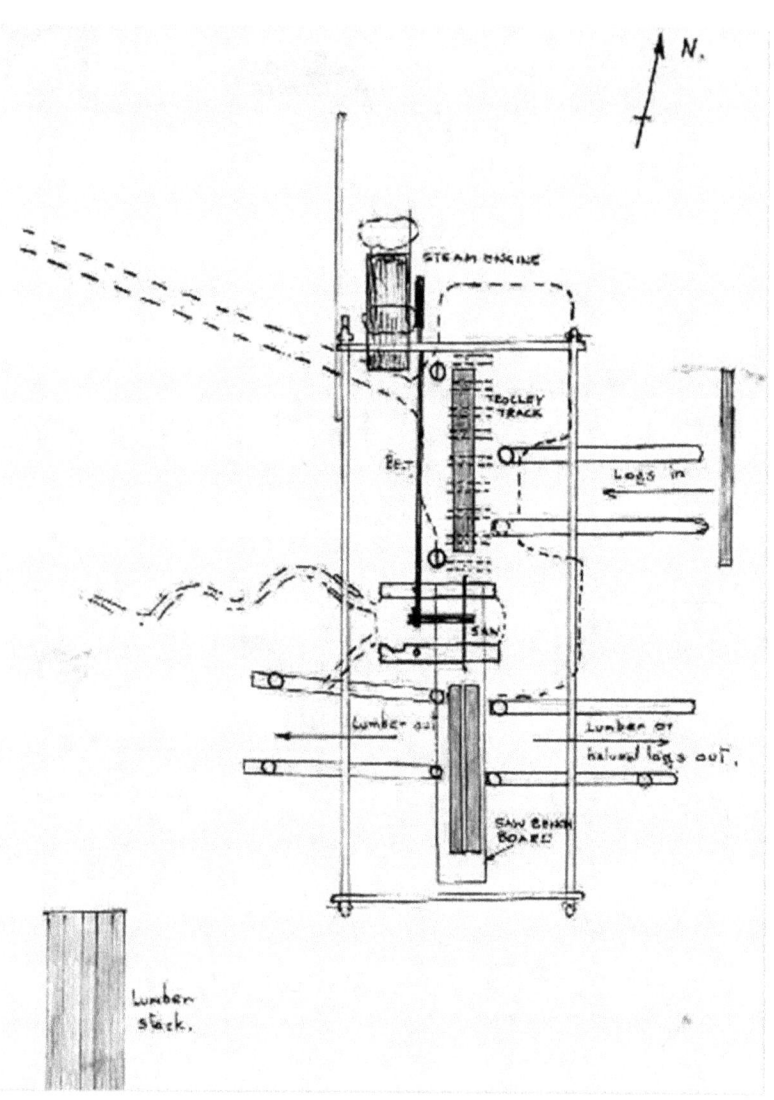

Figure 90. The Newholme sawmill site; suggested reconstruction, 1992, showing the layout and process. Drawn by J.B. Asha.

By the 1980s, I had also recorded or had students record, a variety of buildings and sites in New England that were under threat or little known. One was a pisé building (perhaps a dairy) built in the 1860s at Arding, near Armidale (**Figure 91**). There were also other locations, such as a ruined stone house near Bundarra Road F**igures 92–95**) and a pisé house called 'Eversleigh' at Saumarez Ponds, west of Armidale (**Figures 96 and 97**).

Figure 91. Pisé building at Arding, near Armidale, showing its condition in 1987, after over a century. Note the cracked wall. With Arnold Goode. Photograph by Luke Godwin.

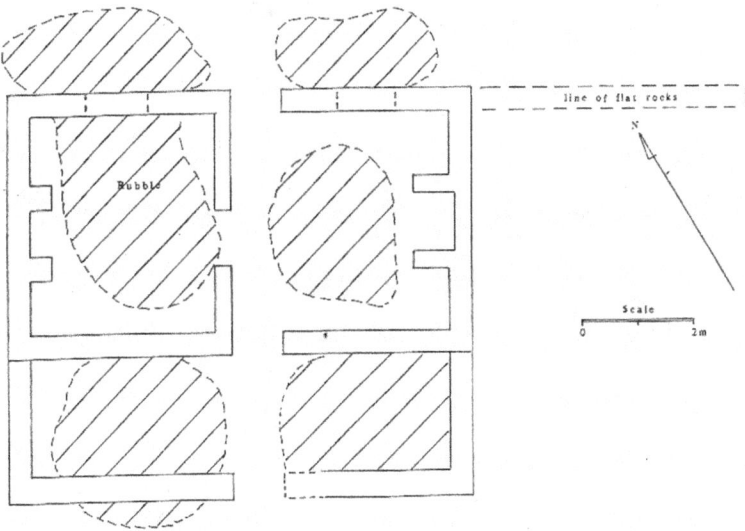

Figure 92. Stone cottage near Bundarra Road, west of Armidale. Parish of Butler, County Sandon, Portion 41. Approximate grid reference: 4.59800YE 12.22460YN. Although not shown, there seems to have been a veranda on its northern side. Surveyed and drawn by John Appleton in 1988.

Figure 93. Front elevation of the house ruin shown in Figure 92. Surveyed and drawn by John Appleton in 1988.

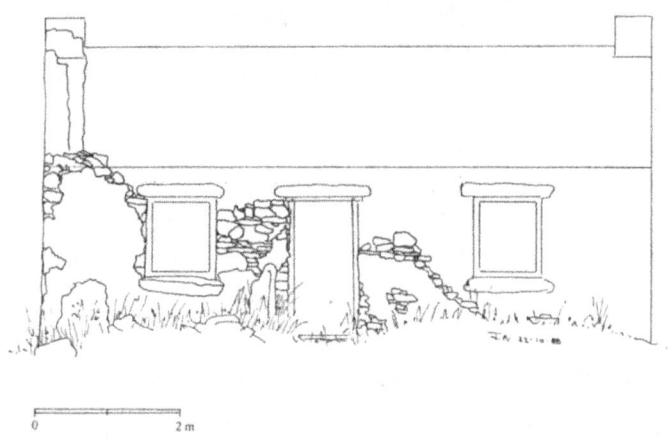

Figure 94. Proposed reconstruction of the front of house ruin shown in Figure 92, Surveyed and drawn by John Appleton in 1988.

Figure 95. House at Loch-an-Eillan, Inverness-shire, Scotland. Compare with the proposed reconstruction in Figure 94. A former farmhouse, now a tourist information centre.

Another student of mine, Bruce Veitch, conducted an archaeological survey of Saumarez Ponds, west of Armidale. It included a number of buildings and sites but the illustrations were poor photocopies and very few photographs seem to have survived. Even the date that it was done is uncertain, although 1982 is probable. One of the main buildings was a house called 'Eversleigh' but a plan made of it is difficult to comprehend.

Overall, although a lot of fieldwork and other work was done, poor record-keeping has limited its subsequent use. A similar sad record exists of the gold-mining town of Melrose, which was situated on the right bank of Postman's Creek, some 23 miles from Uralla and 28 miles from Armidale and existed for only 2 years, from 1889 to 1890. Although its existence was so brief, there were approximately 500 people resident there in December 1889. There were four hotels, a boarding house, an eating house, a police station, a public school with a schoolmaster and 50 pupils, 3 large stores, 2 blacksmiths, a wheelwright's shop, a hairdresser and cigar and fancy goods emporium, 2 bakers, a butcher, a cordial manufacturer, the mine manager, as well as others. In spite of all this, the town died when the gold ran out and the buildings were removed for reuse elsewhere.

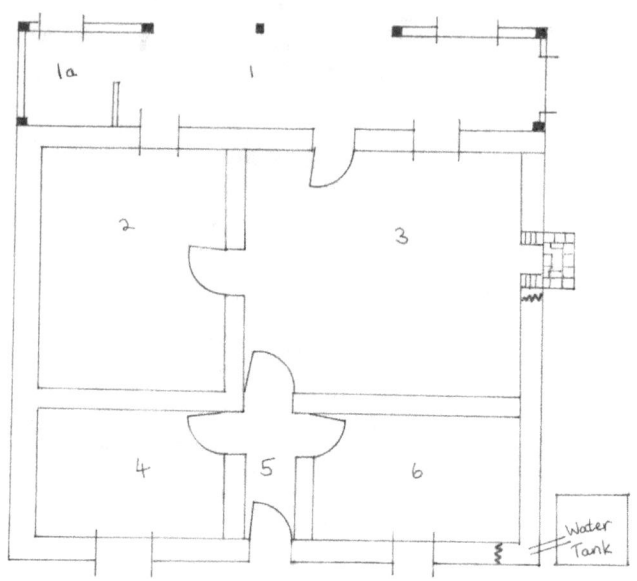

Figure 96. 'Eversleigh', a pisé house at Saumarez Ponds, west of Armidale. North at the top. Plan by Bruce Veitch.

Figure 97. 'Eversleigh', the pisé house at Saumarez Ponds, from the north. Probably in 1982. Photograph by Graham Connah.

In June 1988, a cistern was accidentally uncovered outside the back door of the UNE Vice Chancellor's official university residence 'Trevenna'. Professor Nichol was Vice Chancellor at the time and he and his wife were very understanding while I and a student investigated the top of the feature. We then covered it up again because I had no state permit to excavate it and I was already committed to other time-consuming work. The house was built in the 1890s, so the cistern must have dated from that time or later.

In 1987, I edited and published a sixth ASHA Journal and in 1988 did a special issue for the Bicentennial Year, after which I gave up the editing. Judy Birmingham and her Sydney friends took it over.

19.

Fieldwork and Excavations in Uganda

The year 1988 brought a pleasant surprise to another matter. John Alexander contacted me with the news that John Sutton, the director of a British Research Institute (the BIEA) in East Africa, situated in Nairobi, Kenya, but with a head office in London, was looking for someone to run a field research project in Uganda. Alexander, impressed by my work at Qasr Ibrim, told me that he had recommended me for the job. It was unpaid but BIEA would provide logistical support such as transport, staff and field equipment, if I could fund air travel to Kenya and other field expenses in East Africa.

This required another Australian Research Grants Council application by me but it was successful and in December 1988 I flew to Nairobi to begin the project, taking New Zealander Andrew Piper, a UNE MA student, with me as an assistant. Uganda was in a poor state at this time. After years of Idi Amin's dictatorship and subsequent political instability, the Ugandan Army had taken over, led by Museveni, one of its officers. He was attempting his own form of democracy and there was optimism about the future amongst Ugandans.

Andrew Piper and I spent Christmas and New Year checking equipment in Nairobi and saw a little of Kenya archaeology and its context, assisted by Andrew Reid, a PhD student from Cambridge who had been excavating in Uganda and was familiar with the problems there.

Early in January 1989, the three of us set out for Uganda in a BIEA Land Rover, with Thaddayo, a Luo from western Kenya, as a driver and mechanic. We overnighted in a hotel at Kisumu on the eastern shore of Lake Victoria, where I stupidly forgot and left behind all my travellers' cheques, my source of funds and we lost a lot of time going back for them. Even the memory of my mistake is still an embarrassment after many years, but I must have had a lot on my mind that morning.

We went to the border a second time and after some delay got into Uganda and reached Kampala by evening. There we managed to get accommodation at Namirembe, a guesthouse run by the Anglican Church of Uganda. It had no electricity or water but managed with oil lamps, as far as I can remember and with roof tanks for water and was using a couple of pit toilets. It was run by very resourceful people. We spent some days there while we dealt with the research bureaucracy of the Ugandan government and met up with Ephraim Kamuhangire, of the Uganda Museum, who was to work with us during our fieldwork.

While in Kampala, we visited the royal tombs of the Kabakas at Kasubi in part of the city. It was a massive building of wood and thatch that was destroyed by fire in 2020. We also visited Entebbe on the shore of Lake Victoria to the south and photographed ourselves at the Ugandan Equator (**Figure 99**). All the roads seem to have disintegrated, even the one through Jinja to the border with Kenya was virtually non-existent and those in remoter areas were to prove very difficult.

Figure 98. Me in the field, Kenya, 1989.

Figure 99. Uganda research team at Equator 1989. Left-right: Peter Bisaso, me, Ephraim Kamuhangire, Thaddayo Owuora.

Our first task was to visit known archaeological sites in Uganda, including earthworks at Bigo and Munsa and also at Ntusi, where Andrew Reid had been excavating in what I regarded as primitive conditions. He seemed to be doing this in conjunction with John Sutton. We transported Andrew Reid back to Ntusi to continue with his work. I was mainly interested in the site of Kibiro, however, where an excavation of two test holes by Belgians Hiernaux and Maquet in 1957 had shown there were deep deposits. The site lay on the eastern shore of Lake Albert, at the bottom of a very high and steep escarpment (of over 900 metres), with no road access.

Also, because it was a salt-making site, the soil was very salty and could not produce plant food, which had to be obtained from a market at Kigorobya on the plateau above. After an initial visit to Kibiro, I decided to camp at Kigorobya, where we were able to make ourselves comfortable in the Village Head's compound that was adjacent to the police station. We used tents that had been supplied by BIEA in Nairobi, a local boy brought us water from a nearby stream each day and Andrew Piper proved to be an excellent and imaginative cook.

Nevertheless, the walk down the escarpment each morning and worse still the climb back up each evening proved to be both very time-consuming and very tiring. We could travel to the top of the escarpment or return from there by Land Rover but excavating a test-hole at Kibiro was difficult because of the time taken by travel each day. I think we spent two weeks or so on the task. We got a good deep section (**Figure 104**) and collected samples for radiocarbon dating.

Fortunately, Andrew Piper was not only a good archaeological assistant but also got on well with all the Ugandans we met. On one occasion, a woman in labour was carried up the escarpment on a folded deckchair by Kibiro villagers and we took her in the Land Rover to the clinic in Kigorobya, where she was safely delivered.

At another time, we attended a meeting of local men at Kigorobya, where they told us about the suffering of recent years and their gratitude for present improvement, including our visit. We were much helped by a Kibiro man who seemed better educated than others from his village and more successful. He fished on Lake Albert and owned his own boat, but was unwell. Indeed, when I returned a year later I was told that he had died, apparently of stomach cancer and his boat lay abandoned on the shore at Kibiro. I cannot now even remember his name.

During this first work in Uganda, we also met a friendly educated man who was some sort of government official but by the time of our second Ugandan visit he was dead, apparently killed by a hand grenade thrown at him but I never learnt any details and, again, I cannot remember his name.

After excavating at Kibiro, we did some fieldwork to the south-west of Lake Albert in the Lake George and Queen Elizabeth National Park area, with an armed guard insisted on by the National Parks Department and paid by me. Finally, we went to the far south of Uganda to visit the Ankole capital site at Bweyorere which Merrick Posnansky had excavated in the 1950s. This was a mistake, the site was too late and therefore useless from my point of view, the roads there were the worst we had experienced, there was nowhere to stay and the only available food was suspect. I think that we slept in the open at the site and by the next day, I had developed dysentery.

Worse was to come, returning to Kampala we found John Sutton there and expecting to travel back to Nairobi with us, although he had not forewarned us of his intentions. This included a visit to an old expatriate friend of his, while I struggled with a worsening illness. Back in Nairobi, my condition worsened and an expatriate doctor diagnosed it as Shigella Dysentery. I could eat very little and was soon too weak to fly to Singapore to meet Beryl there as intended. I had to reschedule our flights, eventually travelling some two weeks later, as far as I remember.

In Nairobi, we met Roland Oliver, who was visiting and he was sympathetic to my problem. Back in Armidale, I saw my own doctor, who said that he wondered why I did such things, I replied that I did them for the same reason that he did what he did: because I was good at it.

In 1989, I published an interim report on Kibiro, a long-delayed paper with Sam Freeth about the stones used at sites in Borno and a book review. Otherwise, I spent the year preparing for another season in Uganda, for which I think I had obtained more funding from the Australian Research Grants Council. I had reached the age of 55 and my back, damaged by many years of fieldwork and made worse by the Reddestone Creek excavation, required visits to a very good osteopath in Armidale and daily exercises.

I was due for study leave again in 1990 and I decided to do a much larger excavation at Kibiro while I was able, as well as further fieldwork in other parts of Uganda. My intention was to analyse the excavated material in Kampala, at the Uganda Museum, but to finish the year in Cambridge with relevant research and publication preparation. Andrew Piper wanted to finish his MA at UNE, so was unable to come with me but, on the advice of Mike Morwood, I took Christine Burke as an assistant. She had just completed an Honours thesis at UNE on faunal analysis and it was hoped that she would be able to change from the analysis of Australian fauna, at which she had done well, to the analysis of African fauna.

Beryl was also coming with me to Uganda, so arranging for a female assistant was not inappropriate, although in Uganda there were some people who thought that I merely had a Senior Wife and a Junior Wife, even after I told them that this was not the case.

However, before leaving Australia we arranged to meet Christine for lunch at The Rocks in Sydney, where we told her about the conditions she would have to face, including an AIDS epidemic that was then almost out of control in Africa. At the end of the year, Beryl and I flew to Nairobi, where we stayed for a few days at a National Park to its north and then spent Christmas with the Suttons.

Christine joined us in Nairobi in early January, looking a little lost, but she had grown up in the South Australian bush, was obviously tough and soon adapted to the conditions. We stayed in the rather poor but pleasant conditions of the BIEA visitor accommodation and then spent a week or so checking the camping and field equipment that BIEA was providing us. Some of this needed repair or replacement and this took time to do.

Eventually, we set off in the Land Rover with Thaddayo doing most of the driving and we overnighted at Kisumu as in the previous year. In Kampala, it took some days to deal with the government requirements and then we travelled to Kigorobya and set up a camp there again. This time I was determined to live in tents at Kibiro during the excavation but maintain a base-camp at Kigorobya looked after by Thaddayo, who would supply us with food from the local market several times a week, by bringing it by Land Rover to the top of the escarpment. I would then send a couple of my workmen up to carry it down to us at Kibiro.

To establish the camp at Kibiro, we would carry what we could down the escarpment but most of our loads would be driven by Thaddayo to Butiaba, reachable by road, further north on the eastern shore of Lake Albert and brought by a boat with an outboard motor to Kibiro. It was a good plan but proved to be difficult to implement. The night before these arrangements were to be put into action there was heavy rain at Kigorobya that saturated our stores, particularly the dry food, because the tent leaked so badly.

On the day that we were to set up at Kibiro, we walked down the escarpment satisfactorily, although Beryl fell over once, but we waited hours for the boat to arrive. Eventually, it did come and we managed to set up camp at a convenient location before dark and to get something to eat. It had been a difficult day but we had done everything intended.

Excavations at Kibiro lasted until sometime in March, with several sections completed, mainly in deep deposits. Adopting an American technique I had read about, I tackled the deposit in one cutting (Cutting III: See **Figures 105 and 106**) horizontally rather than with the usual vertical approach. That is to say, I first dug a hole to expose the stratification in the section that I was then able to excavate layer by layer.

In this way, we avoided the difficult problem of recognising layer changes as we excavated, usually a difficult task in African soils. We sieved all the spoil and, during excavation and sieving, recovered a massive amount of pottery. There were also some hearths and one inhumation burial. I was assisted by

Christine Burke and Ephraim Kamuhangire, who had now become the Director of the Uganda Museum.

Also from the Museum was a younger man, Peter Bisaso, who worked well at the excavation. I had some of the Kibiro villagers as a labour force, perhaps ten or so in number. At breakfast one morning, I was confronted by a group of soldiers and their guns: some of my workmen had not paid their taxes and were to be arrested and taken away.

Fortunately, I was able to bail them out and pay their taxes, which I subsequently deducted from their wages and all ended well. My back, however, gave me pain at times and discomfort every day, although painkillers and exercise usually kept it in control. Only one day occurred when I was unable to work and had to leave Christine and Peter to run the excavation. In addition to excavating, we also surveyed the Kibiro salt-making area and made a detailed plan of it, including the adjacent hot spring in a deep valley at the base of the escarpment (**Figures 100–106**).

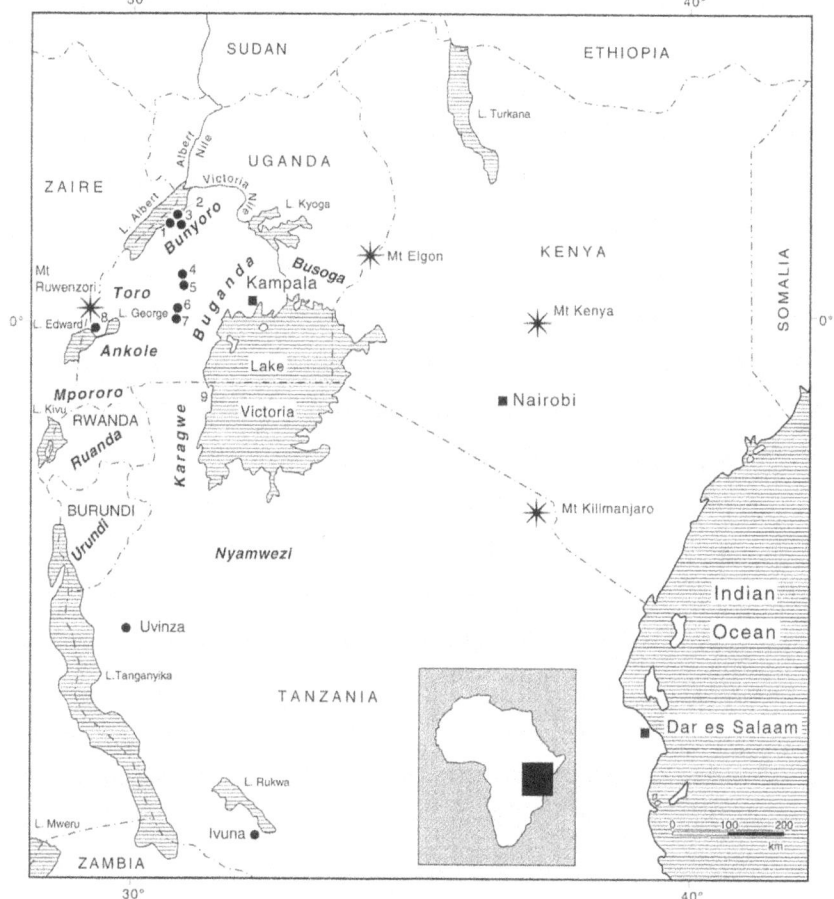

Figure 100. East Central Africa, showing modern political divisions and (in bold) nineteenth-century Interlacustrine kingdoms.1. Kibiro. 2. Butiaba. 3. Kigorobya. 4. Munsa. 5. Mubende. 6. Bigo. 7. Ntusi 8. Katwe. Drawn by Douglas Hobbs.

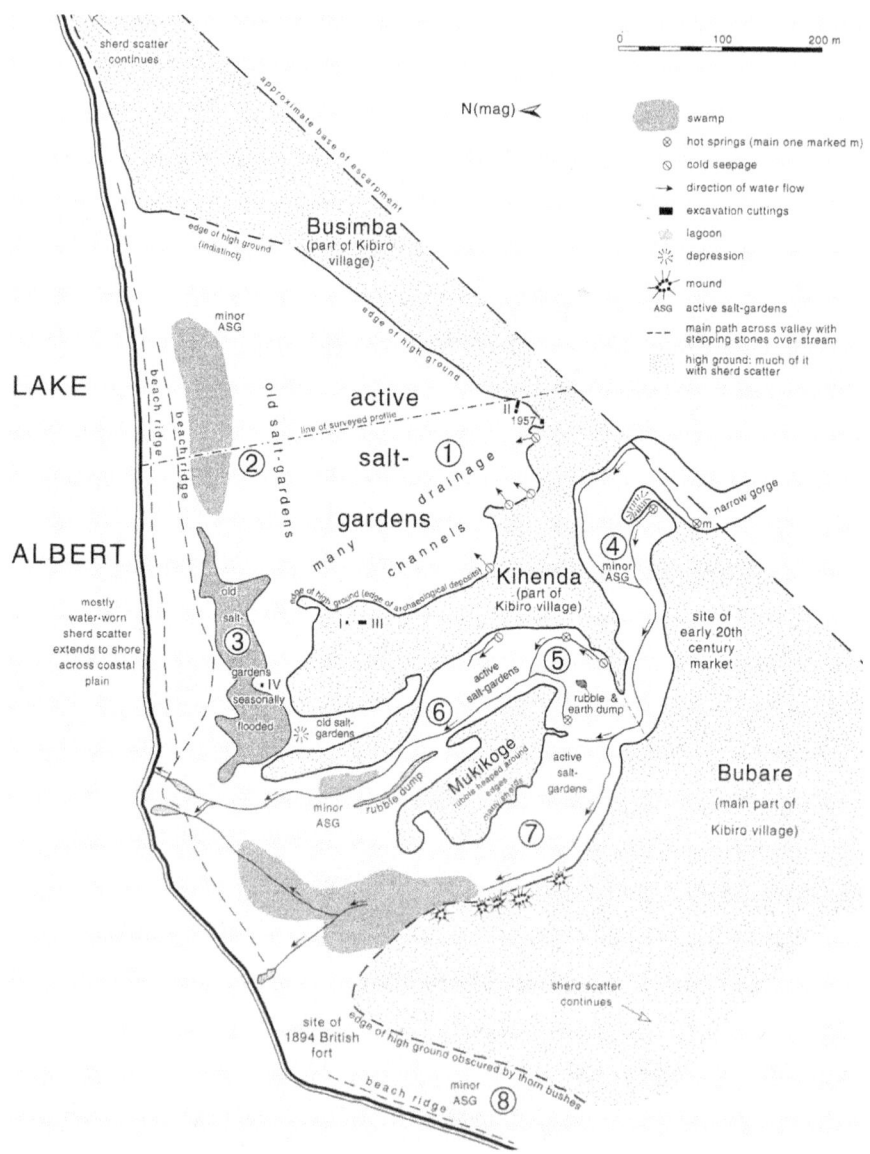

Figure 101. Kibiro, the plan of the salt-making area, surveyed in June 1990, showing the location of 1990 excavations I–IV and one of the 1957 test holes.

Figure 102. A Kibiro woman scraping up salty earth in one of the Kibiro salt-gardens, January 1989. Photograph by Andrew Piper.

Figure 103. Kibiro village and escarpment from a boat on Lake Albert, February 1990. The salt-gardens are in the foreground.

Figure 104. Kibiro excavation, February 1989. Cutting I, the base of Spit 14, near the bottom of the deposit. From north-east, with Andrew Piper.

Figure 105. Kibiro Cutting III, excavation strategy. At work on Area C, Unit 19, March 1990. From south.

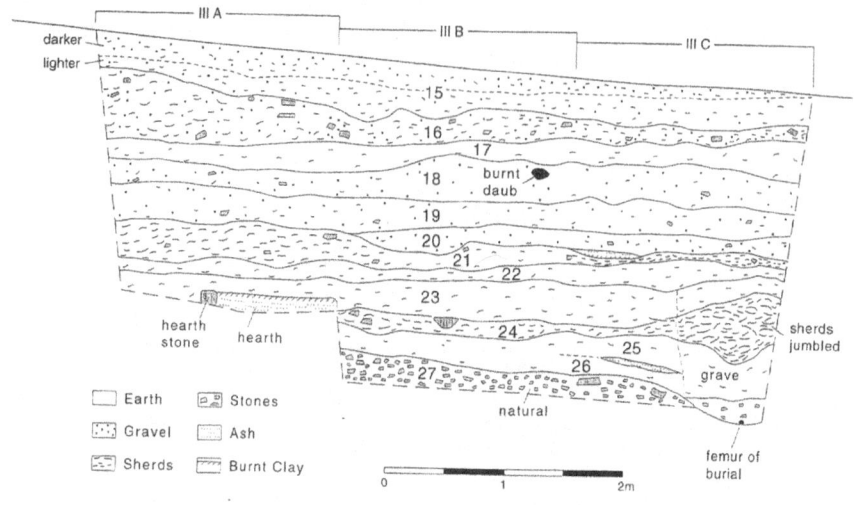

Figure 106. Kibiro excavation 1990, Cutting III, west section.

Other activities during and after the excavation cannot be forgotten. One was feeding ourselves as well as possible, at which we were very successful considering the conditions (**Figure 107**). Another was analysing the artefacts, bones and other evidence from the excavation. This was done in the Uganda Museum, after the excavation and needed all the excavated materials to be carried up the escarpment by our workmen and then transported in the Land Rover to Kampala (**Figure 108–111**). It was remarkable how much we accomplished with such a small workforce.

Figure 107. Kibiro: dinner in a tent. L-R: Beryl Connah, Christine Bourke, Ephraim Kamuhangire, Peter Bisaso. 1990, probably March. Photograph by Graham Connah.

Figure 108. Examining pottery and bones in the Uganda Museum, Kampala. 1990, probably March. L-R: Pamela Grace, Peter Bisaso, unidentified person, Beryl Connah. Photograph by Graham Connah. The unidentified person might be a brief BIEA student who did independent archaeological fieldwork in the Lake Victoria area during this time but whose name has been forgotten and who was not part of my Uganda project.

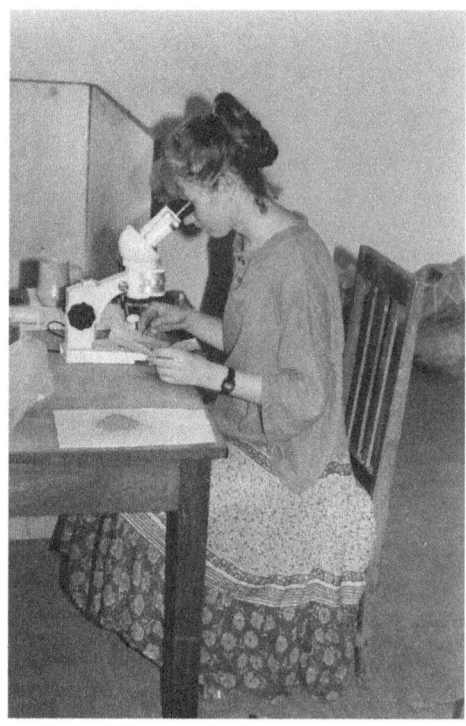

Figure 109. Christine Bourke using a microscope to examine bones from Kibiro, in the Uganda Museum, Kampala. 1990, probably March. Photograph by Graham Connah.

Figure 110. Kibiro, March 1990. Workforce probably at the end of the excavation.
Front, L-R: Peter Bisaso, Beryl Connah, Graham Connah,
Erika Bitaagase (Chairman RC Kibiro) and Ephraim Kamuhangire behind him.
Workmen and Christine Bourke further back.

Figure 111. Loading the Land Rover at the Uganda Museum, Kampala. Probably a photograph by Pamela Grace, in June 1990.

Our campsite by the lake proved to be a good choice, we bought fish from the lake and got meat and vegetables from Kigorobya. The tilapia were good, the catfish less so and the meat needed a lot of cleaning. We had to eat a lot of rather poor sweet potatoes and many bananas, some of which were mutoki and needed cooking. Cooking was over an open fire, although firewood supplies were limited and we had to use some every evening to boil water from the lake to make it safe to drink the next day. I got my workmen to dig a deep latrine pit (of about 4 metres) at the campsite and to construct a washing place, in which each of us was limited to one bucket of water each day and the use of a plastic sponge. It was also necessary to have a piece of stone to stand on, to keep one's feet out of the mud.

On one occasion, we were visited by the police who thoughtfully came down the escarpment to see if we were alright. We were also visited by John Sutton, who brought Rowland Oliver with him. We had problems nearing the end of the excavation, Christine got sick and Beryl spent a bad final night apparently caused by dried milk that had deteriorated.

Nevertheless, we were able to leave the campsite on the intended day and pull back to Kigorobya. We then travelled with Thaddayo to Nairobi, staying for a night at Kisumu, where we were able to have baths at the hotel, only to discover that we had lost so much weight that our pelvic bones made sitting in the bath painful. Back at the BIEA in Nairobi, we lived in John Sutton's house nearby because he and his wife were on leave in Britain and I sorted out the excavation records and photographs. Christine was able to spend time with a woman from the Kenya Museum who helped her with the Kibiro faunal analysis.

Also, I think that Gilbert Oteyo, a BIEA technician, started some illustration work on the pottery. According to my memory, we were in Nairobi during April and May but in June we returned to Uganda where Beryl and I, with Thaddayo and Ephraim, did fieldwork to the south of Lake Albert, in the Queen Elizabeth National Park and adjacent areas. We left Christine in Nairobi to continue her work on the Kibiro faunal analysis and because her health still seemed uncertain. We camped during this fieldwork and at night could hear a hippopotamus grazing outside the tent. I assumed it was harmless and only later learnt that they can be very dangerous if disturbed.

During the fieldwork, we had an armed guard from the Uganda National Parks Department paid by me, as on the previous occasion that we had worked in this area. Indeed, I think it was at this time that we were threatened by an elephant that objected to the Land Rover but our guard fired one round over its head and it took off at speed. We were back in Nairobi by August and, with Christine, we visited Gedi (**Figure 112**) and several other sites on the Kenyan coast. We even managed a trip to Zimbabwe, where we visited the Great Zimbabwe site (**Figures 113–114**).

Figure 112. Entrance to the Palace at the town site of Gedi, on the coast of Kenya, 1990. Beryl is the scale.

Figure 113. Great Zimbabwe, view of the tower within the Great Enclosure, 1990. Photograph by Graham Connah.

Figure 114. Great Zimbabwe, G1 entrance to the Great Enclosure, with characteristic rounded wall-ends, 1990. Photograph by Graham Connah.

After that, we flew to Britain in September, where Edna Miller had yet again found us good accommodation in Cambridge. This time it was in an apartment in Mawson Place, a passageway off Mawson Road, at the side of a pub called: 'The Live Let Live'. Christine spent a few days with us while she worked on her report about the Kibiro bones. She then went off at her own expense and travelled in England and Scotland. I only ever saw her once again, many years later, at Cooleman Court, Weston, Canberra. She was then apparently living in Canberra and this was sometime in the 2000s, I think. I did not recognise her but she recognised me and told me that the Ugandan experience had changed her life, intending a compliment to me, I think.

Beryl and I stayed in Cambridge until January or February 1991, while I worked on a book about the Ugandan project. I particularly remember New Year's Eve 1990, at the 'Live Let Live', where the friendly proprietor gave everyone a glass of wine. He was a kind man who made his pub popular with the residents of the area. The day we left it had snowed and we had to leave our rented television set with him, for return, its owners were unable to collect it because of the snow.

In 1990, I produced an interim report on the Ugandan work and completed a paper with Andrew Piper and Ephraim Kamuhangire on the salt-making process at Kibiro. Another paper on Uganda was published in 1991 in *Antiquity*. I think that it was in 1991 that I attended a conference in Mombasa and presumably presented a paper there. Otherwise, most of my research and writing time was spent on a book about Kibiro and other sites in Uganda, including another working visit to Cambridge with Beryl during the long vacation of 1991–1992.

The resulting Kibiro book was published by BIEA. Produced and published in Britain, it eventually appeared in 1996, by which time I had moved on to other work. 1993 was marked by the publication of a paperback version of *The Archaeology of Australia's History* and a Japanese language translation of the first edition of *African Civilizations*.

20.

Further Fieldwork in Uganda

Beryl and I did more fieldwork in Uganda during the 1993–1994 long vacation. We camped uncomfortably at Butiaba after a group of British commercial expatriates had refused to lend us the camping site that they were not actually using. We looked for more possible archaeological sites along the north-eastern shore of Lake Albert, hiring a boat with an outboard motor as transport. We then turned our attention to the Victoria Nile, further north, camping at the Kabarega National Park there.

By now, we had discovered the value of the jiko, a small stove using charcoal that could be lit with a little kerosine or, using the local method, with some dry grass. Jikos were made from pieces of steel sheeting cut from old large oil drums, so I had two made in Nairobi before going to Uganda. They had a perforated base with supporting legs and a little door beneath, allowing control of the draught. They made cooking and boiling water much more efficient than using an open fire.

When the fieldwork ended, I gave them away to several of our helpers. This fieldwork included a very small excavation to test one of the sites in the Park but it proved very shallow. Our field assistant was again a UNE graduate student, this time a man called Ray Fife (**Figure 115**). I particularly relied on him for recording site locations with a Global Positioning System (GPS) that I had purchased for the Ugandan work.

At that time, they were new and still not very accurate but they were a great improvement on the crude methods of site location that I had previously relied on. As already mentioned, I retired in early 1995, having passed the age of 60 the previous August. After an interim paper on the 1994 Ugandan work, the Kibiro book was published in 1996.

Figure 115. Me and Ray Fife, field assistant in Uganda in 1994. Probably at my UNE retirement party, November 1994.

21.

UNE in 1992 and 1993

In 1992, the university converted a building that had housed a first-year science laboratory into a new department for Archaeology and Palaeoanthropology, which became our third home while I was at UNE. The Maintenance Department did a remarkable job on it, completely gutting the interior and replanning it. It gave us the best working facilities that we could wish for and I was very happy with it (**Figure 116**). It was also at this time that Di Watson, our Administrative Assistant in the Department, died (**Figure 117**).

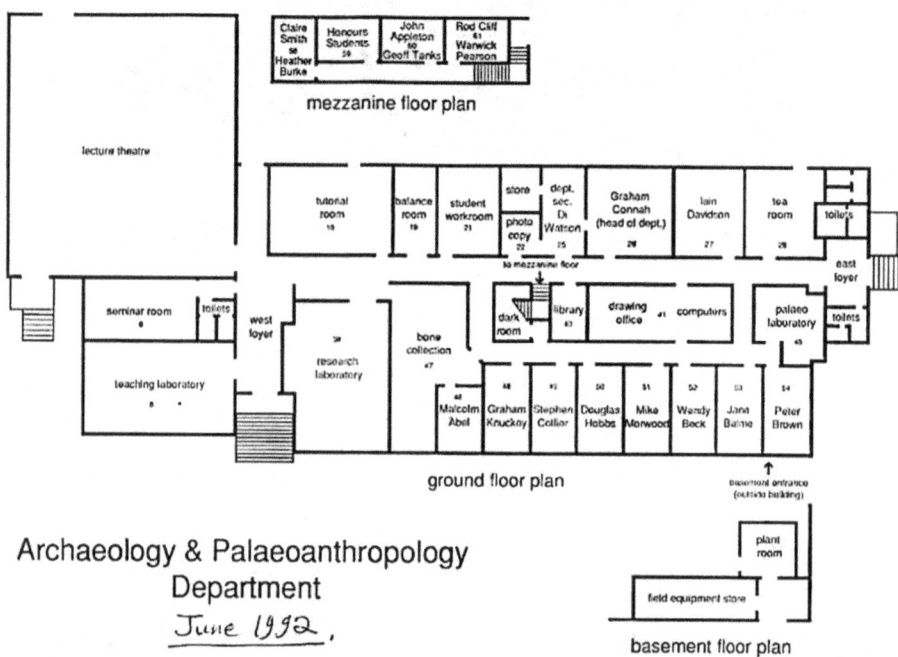

Figure 116. The UNE Department in its third location, before my 1995 retirement.

Tribute

Mrs. Diane Watson

It is with deepest regret that the Department of Archaeology and Palaeoanthropology has to announce the death on 20ᵗʰ July of Mrs Diane Watson, the department's Administrative Assistant. Diane Watson joined the University on November 1970 and was a secretary in the Department of English for ten years. Subsequently she was part-time Administrative Assistant in the Department of Politics for over three years and since December 1984 had been the Administrative Assistant in the Department of Archaeology and Palaeoanthropology.

Any Departmental Administrative Assistant is a key person in the running of an academic department but Di Watson, as we all knew her, was an exception. She had a immense capacity for getting through quantities of work of unimaginable proportions but was always relaxed and helpful to staff and students alike. As a result, she was known, respected, trusted and very much liked by members of staff both in this department and in others, as well as by over two decades of students. As the 'voice on the phone' she was particularly appreciated by external students, who found her ever helpful whatever their problems.

A hard worker, a very capable organizer and administrator, a good personal friend, she will be sadly missed.

Contributed by Professor Graham E Connah, head of Department of Archaeology and Palaeoanthropology.

Figure 117. A tribute to Di Watson, Administrative Assistant, Dept of Arc & Pal, who died 20 July 1993. UNE Smiths Weekly, 30 July 1993.

22.
Limekilns, Tobacco Kilns
and Other Buildings

In September–October 1992, I continued to involve my students in practical field research. This included limekilns and tobacco-drying kilns in the area north of Tamworth (**Figures 118–120**) and recording the chaff-shed and stables at Newholme north of Armidale. Students also recorded the woolshed at Newholme which was unusual because it had originally been a structure at the Armidale showground but had been disassembled and re-erected at Newholme (**Figure 88**). The grain-store and dairy at Newholme were also recorded.

In addition, I extended student investigations to various museum artefacts, including clocks, miners' tools, a hay-mower, a heritage train and other items. These were in the Glen Innes Museum and other museums.

Deposits of limestone are infrequent in the area near Tamworth but there are a number in what is known as 'The Attunga Belt' to its north. These supplied several limekilns near Tamworth.

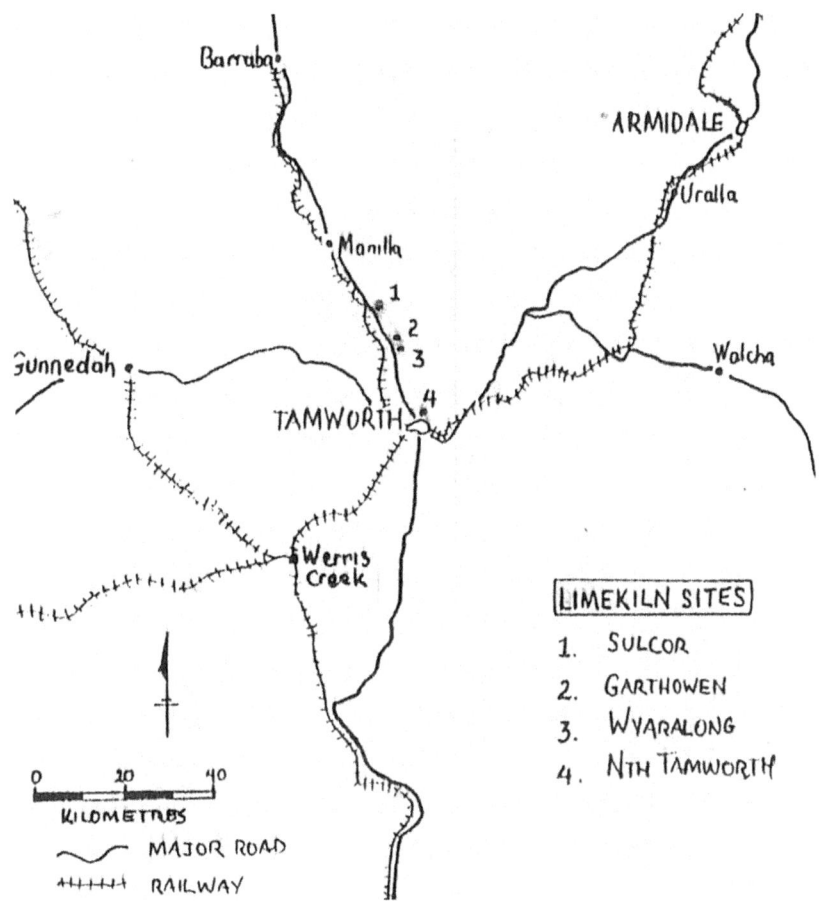

Figure 118. Map of limekilns north of Tamworth, New South Wales. Drawn by Garry Newley, 1992.

*Figure 119. Fire arch at Arklands Limekiln, near Tamworth, Rebecca Hall report,
photograph Garry Newley. Small scale in centimetres.*

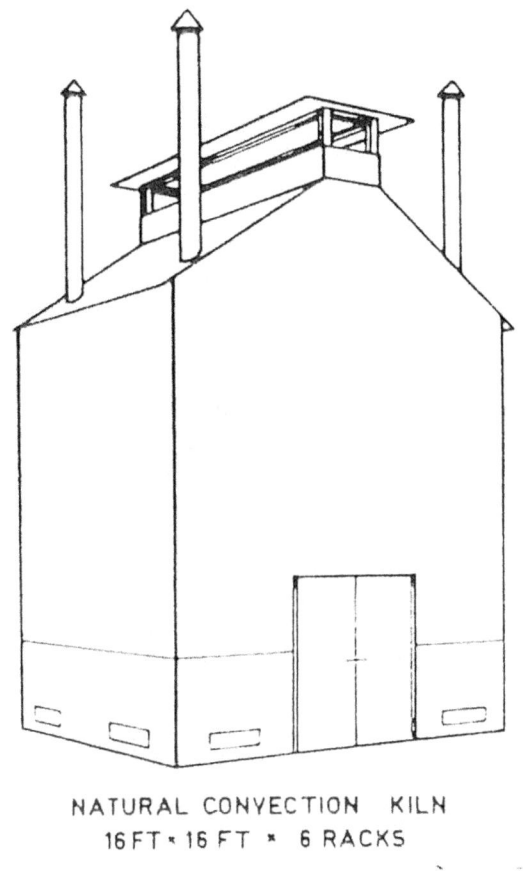

NATURAL CONVECTION KILN
16 FT × 16 FT × 6 RACKS

Figure 120. Reconstruction drawing in 1992 by Melissa Thorpe, of derelict up-draught kiln for drying tobacco, near Tamworth.

23.

Retirement and ANU Conference

When retiring, I told my UNE colleagues that I was going on permanent study leave, particularly to catch up on a lot of writing. In 1995, I was a Visiting Fellow in the Humanities Research Centre at the Australian National University in Canberra, where I had a room. During my year there, I ran a conference on the African archaeological past (**Figure 121**), the papers from which were eventually published in 1998 as *Transformations in Africa: Essays on Africa's later past,* by Leicester University Press. In addition, during this period, I tried to maintain contact with as many other archaeologists as possible (**Figure 122**).

Figure 121. Advertisement for the ANU conference about the African archaeological past, the papers from which were published in 1998
Transformations in Africa: Essays on Africa's later past.

Figure 122. Beryl and I with Rhys Jones and Betty Meehan at the Australian Academy of the Humanities Annual Dinner on 19 November 1992.

During 1995, I also attended the Congress of the Pan-African Association of Prehistory and Related Studies, in Harare, Zimbabwe, giving a paper that was later published. Otherwise, at long last, I wrote up the Bagots Mill excavations, much aided by the analysis work that Sue Pearson had done. This was published as a paper in *Australasian Historical Archaeology* 1994, although dated 1996.

I also published other items, including reviews, but by now a project about Lake Innes House at Port Macquarie was requiring attention. Nevertheless, I decided to have a rest and we spent much of 1996 back in Cambridge in a house rented from an ageing artist who had gone to France to paint. I read for pleasure, attended a dinner at Selwyn celebrating 40 years since my contemporaries and I had come up to Cambridge and visited Oxford, where our rented car was broken into and damaged.

24.

Aksum and Ethiopian Excavation

Most important, however, was a two- or three-week visit that we both made to Ethiopia. This was to see the excavations that David Phillipson was conducting at Aksum (then in their final season) and to go to some other Ethiopian archaeological sites. We flew to Addis Ababa, where we stayed for several days in a hotel and then flew on to Mekelle and Aksum, staying in a hotel at the latter. We were able to spend quite a lot of time at the Aksum excavations but also hired a car with a driver who acted as a guide and took us to other places of interest including the ruins of the 2500-year-old temple at Yeha (**Figures 123–126**).

Unfortunately, we were unable to fit in a visit to the rock-cut churches at Lalibela. An Ethiopian Airways plane, just before our flight back to London, was highjacked and crashed into the Indian Ocean near the Comoro Islands. We were very lucky. Back in Britain, various things were done for the remainder of the year, but we also spent a few very pleasant days in South Wales, staying in a small cottage that Kathleen, my sister and a friend had discovered at Talley near Talley Abbey, a ruined monastery in Carmarthenshire, six miles north of Llandeilo.

The main stelae at Aksum. Ethiopia. 1996.

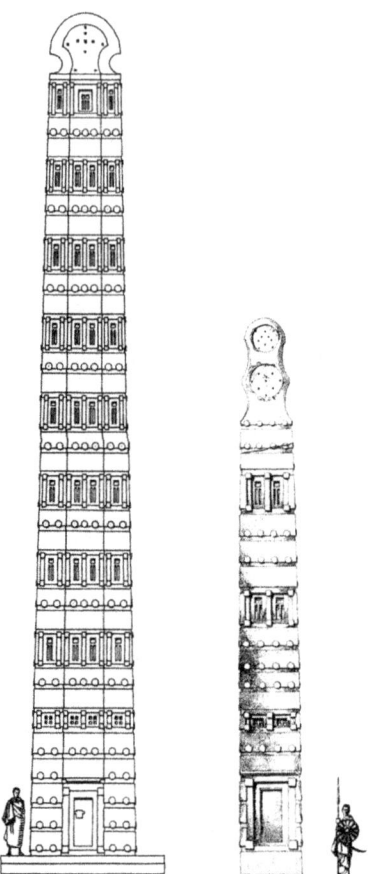

Figure 123. The main stelae at Aksum. Ethiopia. 1996. After Krencker, D. 1913.
Deutsche Aksum-Expedition, Band II. *Georg Reimer, Berlin and Phillipson 1997.* The
monuments of Aksum (based on the work of the Deutsche Aksum-Expedition of 1906).

Figure 124. The false door at the base of the front of the main stela at Aksum. Ethiopia, 1996.

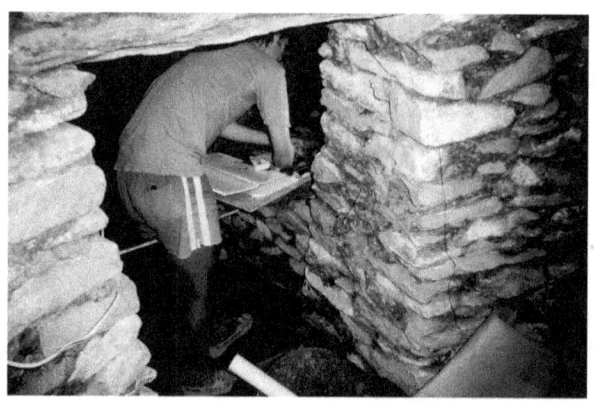

Figure 125. Jess Tipper worked in the chamber of the Tomb of the Brick Arches at Aksum Ethiopia in 1996.

Figure 126. Inside the Yeha Temple, dating from the seventh or sixth century BC. Ethiopia, with guide, 1996.

25.

Uppsala, Sweden and a German Conference

In 1998 and 1999, Beryl and I spent two winters in the snow at Uppsala University in Sweden, invited by Paul Sinclair who had become the Professor of African Archaeology there (**Figure 127**). I did some supervision and lecturing, which was in English, fortunately, used widely at the university. We enjoyed our visits to Uppsala, people were both friendly and kind and the university treated us generously. They could not pay me because of taxation regulations but they paid expenses instead.

For instance, our costs were covered for travel to the Swedish island of Gotland, where we were able to look at some of its archaeology. We also went by rail all the way to northern Norway, which we found had developed a great deal since our visit in the 1960s, as a consequence of the profits from oil. We lived in a university apartment provided to us at no cost and during our first visit conveniently near the Archaeology Department in the centre of Uppsala, although during the second visit, we were further away.

Our first visit was memorable for both the amount of snow and temperatures as low as -19°C, but I cannot remember much about the weather during the second visit. Most importantly, I was able to work on the preparation of a second edition of *African Civilizisations* that required both revision and some rewriting. This involved a lot of computer work with which I was helped by the advice of Aka Johanson, a university technician. Elisabet Greene, secretary and assistant to Paul Sinclair, was also helpful in many other ways (**Figures 128–130**).

Figure 128. Me and Paul Sinclair at the SAFA conference in Calgary, Canada, in 2006.

Figure 128. The Department of Archaeology and Ancient History at Uppsala University, Sweden, in 1999. Photograph by Graham Connah.

Figure 129. Outside of the city walls, Visby, Gotland, in 1999. Photograph by Graham Connah.

Figure 130. Ship burial, Gannarve, Gotland, 1999. Bronze Age. Excavated and restored in 1959. Photograph by Graham Connah.

Also in 1998 Beryl and I attended a Society of Africanist Archaeologists conference held in Frankfurt, Germany and organised by the Johann Goethe University. One of the sessions was held in my honour and was published later by the journal *Azania* (**Figure 131**). A similar publication in my honour was published by ASHA in 2009 as Volume 27 of *The Australasian Journal of Historical Archaeology*.

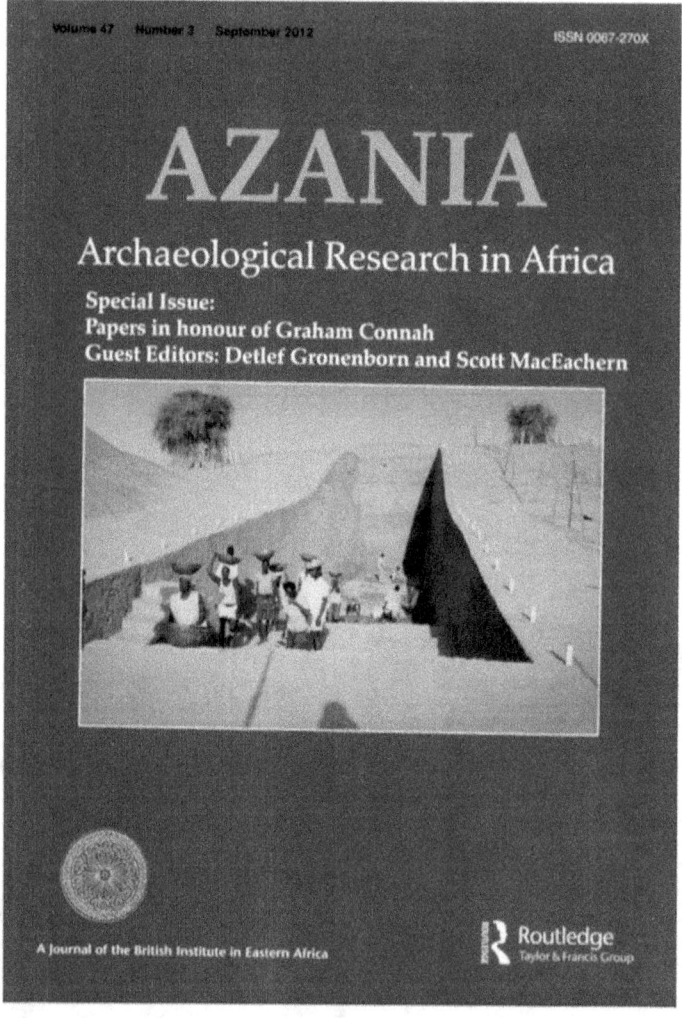

Figure 131. The issue of Azania *in my honour. The photograph on the cover was by Thurstan Shaw, of the Daima VIII excavation in progress.*

26.

Lake Innes, Fieldwork and Excavations

Starting in 1993, the Lake Innes project took much of my time both on-site and with writing. At first, it consisted of a survey and recording, that was published in 1997 as *The archaeology of Lake Innes House: Investigating the visible evidence 1993–1995*. However, I continued to write and publish on a range of other subjects, both African and Australian.

At the end of the 1990s, I obtained an Australian Research Council grant that gave me funding for three years of excavation at Lake Innes, that lasted from 1999 to 2001. I assembled a large workforce that was mostly volunteer, although I did manage to cover expenses for some. The funds I had enabled me to equip the excavation with two motor-driven sieves that I had an engineer specially design and build. Short-range radios were also obtained so that we could communicate between the excavation sites that were some distance from each other. When needed, we used a hired cherry-picker from which we could take vertical photographs (**Figures 132–136**).

Figure 132. Excavation at Lake Innes House, 2000, view from east (Connah, 2007. The same under a different sky? A country estate in nineteenth-century New South Wales. Figure 1.2, Numbers 1, 4, 13).

Figure 133. Lake Innes House excavation, 2000. View from the west of the front door and adjacent rooms. Scale of 2 metres in 20-centimetre divisions.

Figure 134. Lake Innes, 2000. Motor-driven sieves made for the excavation, an Australian design similar to sieves seen in Canada in 1981.

Figure 135. Me at the Lake Innes excavation site, 2001.

Figure 136. Cherry-picker in use for vertical photography at the Lake Innes excavation, 2000.

Each season we were able to include several weeks of analysis work after the excavation that was done at the National Parks and Wildlife base in Port Macquarie. Particularly important for their contributions to the project were: Bryan Asha, Kay Brown, Beryl Connah, Ross Gam, Gillian Goode, Pat Heipertz, Samantha Higgs, Lotta Hillerdal, John Hodgkinson, Sue Hudson, Reinis Kalnins, Deirdre Llewellyn, Bruce McConachy, Samantha McKay, Terry Moore, Rod Mountford, David Pearson, Betty Pinkerton, Paul Rheinberger, Julia Searle, Sue

Singleton, Lindsay Smith, Jean Smith, Robert Tickle, Elizabeth White, Peter White and Sylvia Yates.

Also important was Eric Claussen, the National Parks officer who was responsible for the site. We even had a student from Uppsala (Lotta Hillerdal) who came all the way from Sweden for one season to take part in the excavation.

Overall, the Lake Innes excavations were a great success during the three years in which they were conducted. This was mainly because of the large size of the project that was made possible by the Australian Research Council grant and by the number of people who worked on the site. Also important, however, were the years of surface recording from 1993 to 1995 (**Figure 137**) and the detailed preparations that were made prior to each excavation season. Things had improved greatly since Clybucca in 1972! In 1994, at the time of my impending retirement, students at Lake Innes House presented me with a gold-plated trowel, with reference to Kent Flannery's famous 1982 paper 'The Golden Marshalltown' (**Figure 138**).

The archaeology of
Lake Innes House

Investigating the visible evidence
1993–1995

Edited by
Graham Connah

Published by Connah, Canberra
for the New South Wales National Parks and Wildlife Service
1997

NSW
NATIONAL
PARKS AND
WILDLIFE
SERVICE

Figure 137. Publication of the surface fieldwork before the Lake Innes excavations,
a vital step in the project.

Figure 138. Presentation of the gold-plated trowel at Lake Innes House, 1994. L-R: Kay Brown, me, Deirdre Llewellyn, Beryl Connah. Photograph by Warren Day.

27.

Tasmanian Conference
and Gun Archaeology

In 1999, I attended a conference in Launceston, Tasmania, organised by the University of Tasmania Centre for Tasmanian Historical Studies. The conference was entitled 'Historians and museums: New sites of knowledge'. I read a paper, published in 2000, entitled 'The voice of the artefact', in which I tried to show how artefacts were themselves historical sources.

To do this, I used five examples to demonstrate how artefacts could 'speak' to us. The first was a World War I machine gun, the second an emergency medical kit from the same war probably carried by a stretcher-bearer, the third an early clothes-washing machine, the fourth a nineteenth-century railway locomotive and the fifth a 'bush' mousetrap. I am unsure whether I achieved anything but at least there has been a change in attitudes since the 1950s, when many historians thought medieval archaeology, for instance, was unnecessary because there were so many documents.

In 2002, I collaborated with David Pearson on the first of several papers about historical artillery, which was his main research interest. The initial publication was about a nineteenth-century British Naval gun that I had examined at the Uganda Museum in 1994, during fieldwork in that country. It was entitled 'Artefact of Empire: The tale of a gun' and appeared in *Historical Archaeology*.

The gun's recent history was complicated, but it was significant as an example of gun development at an important stage. It was muzzle-loading but had a rifled barrel, thus showing both conservatism and innovation. Although manufactured in 1870, it had seen action in World War I, when it sank a German vessel on Lake Victoria. It was by then 44 years old and mounted on a converted tug called the *Kavirondo* but sank the other vessel with its fifth shot (**Figures 139 and 140**).

Later, we also published together about a German 88mm gun from World War II and about a World War I gun, a monster 150mm gun stored at the Australian War Memorial in Canberra (**Figures 141 and 142**). These were published respectively in 2010 and 2013. Eventually, David Pearson gained employment at the Australian War Memorial (museum) in Canberra.

Figure 139. British Naval gun outside the Uganda Museum in Kampala in 1994, seen in the recoil position. Photograph by Graham Connah.

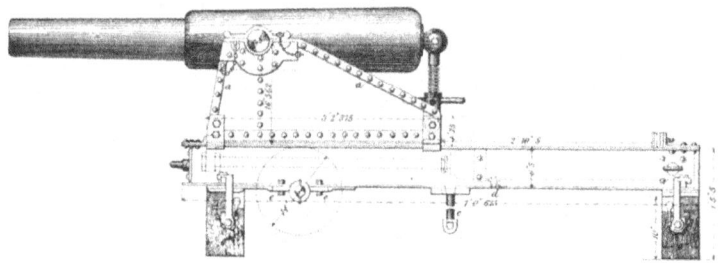

Figure 140. Illustration of 1879 showing how the 9-pounder Mark 1 rifled muzzle-loading gun was mounted for Naval service. This was for an 8-hundredweight gun but the design was similar for the 6-hundredweight version. It is suggested that the Kampala gun might have been older than the carriage and slide.

Figure 141. World War II German 88mm gun, in the Puckapunyal Army Museum, Victoria.

Figure 142. World War I German 150mm gun (with other guns). Canberra War Memorial Store, 2013, with David Pearson.

28.

Mike Morwood Discovers *Homo Floresiensis*

In 2003, Mike Morwood brought the University of New England Archaeology and Palaeoanthropology Department into the international limelight with his discovery of the skull of *Homo floresiensis* in Indonesia. Quickly nicknamed 'The Hobbit', after J.R.R. Tolkien's 1937 novel which was the basis of three popular films at about the time of the skull's discovery, it caused a storm of debate in which its status as a unique species was seriously questioned.

However, other similar skeletal material was subsequently found and Morwood's opinion was supported by Peter Brown, also of the UNE department and by others. Mike was so dedicated to research that he neglected his health and he sadly died in 2013 in Darwin at age 62, when he was on his way to visit his Indonesian colleagues yet again. I last saw him several years before that when I invited him to give a lecture to the Canberra Archaeological Society for whom I was then arranging their programme.

At a dinner hosted by the Society beforehand, I asked him whether he was going to retire and he strongly replied that he had no intention of doing so. He was by then a professor at the University of Wollongong. I always encouraged him in his research and Mike acknowledged my support. In response, he helped for brief periods at the excavations of Saumarez Homestead and Lake Innes House. He was also a good and successful supervisor of Honours students and their theses. John Mulvaney once told me that when he supervised Mike's PhD research at the ANU, Mike was no trouble at all, he just got on with it. It was a privilege to have known Mike Morwood.

29.

Conference in Botswana

In 2005, I attended the Twelfth conference of the Pan-African Archaeological Association (formerly known as the Pan-African Congress of Prehistory and Quaternary Studies) held at the museum in Gaborone, Botswana. This was attended by both Africans and delegates from other parts of the world. I also saw something of the university there (**Figures 143–144**). I was impressed by Botswana but my visit was limited to Gaborone because my health prevented me from going on a demanding fieldtrip to the Okavango Delta in the far north.

The son of Seretse Khama, 1921–1980, (the first president of Botswana) and his English wife, Ruth Williams, whom he had married in 1948 and survived resulting difficulties, was Vice President at the time of my visit, I was told. Botswana seemed to be more successful than some other African countries, with an economy supported by cattle and diamonds and an apparently stable government. Appropriately, outside the museum in Gaborone was a bronze statue of a cow and a herdsman. During the early years of my retirement, Beryl and I also travelled to America, Canada and New Zealand, in the latter case, two or three times.

In the early 1990s, we even went sailing for a week on the Great Barrier Reef in northern Queensland, with Alan and Julie who had the necessary expertise to handle the yacht that we hired.

Figure 143. Some of the delegates at the Gaborone conference, Botswana, in 2005, outside the museum. Photograph by Graham Connah.

Figure 144. Part of the university in Gaborone, Botswana, 2005. Photograph by Graham Connah.

30.

Greenland and Back

In 2007, Beryl and I went on a cruise from Britain to Greenland, returning via Ireland. We then flew back to Singapore and Australia. Below is a selection of photographs taken during this journey (**Figures 145–150**).

Figure 145. British 9.2-inch Mark I Heavy Siege Howitzer, Imperial War Museum, London. My father served on similar guns with the Royal Garrison Artillery during World War I.

Figure 147. The centre of Kirkwall, Orkney, from the top of the Bishop's Palace tower.

Figure 147. Turf-roofed buildings in Torshavn, Faroe Islands.

Figure 148. Ice off the west coast of Greenland.

Figure 149. According to its markings, probably a Russian 18-pounder gun, captured during the Crimean War. Cork, Ireland.

Figure 150. Armenian church of St Gregory, Singapore. Built 1835, modified 1853. This is the oldest church in Singapore.

31.

More Writing and Publishing

My writing and publication continued after Lake Innes and included a book that I had wanted to write for some time. This was an introduction to African archaeology and I called it *Forgotten Africa: An introduction to its archaeology*. It was published in London and New York, in hardback, paperback and e-book, in 2004 but sales were disappointing, although during the following years, it was translated into German (two editions) and into French, Italian and Portuguese.

I also tried to arrange for an Arabic translation but a man at Khartoum University, that I corresponded with, gave up after a short time. It was an important book because, as suggested by the title, it emphasised our knowledge of the African past as provided by archaeology, rather than concentrating on the limited approach of historians. It was also important because it tried to reach as wide a readership as possible (**Figures 151 and 152**).

Figure 151. An illustration in Forgotten Africa. *Aksumite copper coin, with the Christian cross and a gold inlaid spot at its centre. Photograph from David Phillipson.*

Figure 152. An illustration in Forgotten Africa. *Terracotta head from Nok, Nigeria, 500 BC–200 AD. Photograph from Bernard Fagg.*

Numerous other publications followed. One of the most important was: *The same under a different sky? A country estate in nineteenth-century New South Wales,* published in 2007 by BAR, Oxford. This was a comprehensive account of the Lake Innes excavations, incorporating contributions from some of those who had taken part in the work.

In 2019, I also published the Saumarez Homestead excavations of the 1980s, with the title *Vestiges of the past: Excavating Saumarez Old Homestead.* David Pearson helped me to write up the 1986 Qasr Ibrim excavation, that was published in 2016 by BAR, Oxford. Autobiographical writing got attention in 2011 with *Prelude: Growing up in the middle of the twentieth century*, published privately, but without more details about my seafaring maternal grandfather that were discovered too late to include (but an addendum was added). Another piece of autobiographical writing was *Cambridge to Lake Chad: Life in archaeology 1956–1971,* published by Archaeopress, Oxford, in 2018.

At a conference of the (American) Society for Historical Archaeology, held in York (UK) in 2000, the archaeological editor for Cambridge University Press agreed with me that much of the writing about archaeology was poor and he suggested that I write a book about the subject. This I did and it was published as *Writing about archaeology*, by Cambridge University Press, in New York, in both hardback and paperback, in 2010 (**Figure 153**).

Figure 153. Me at the book launch of Writing about archaeology, *May 2010. In the ANU University bookshop.*

Other publications included a third edition of *African Civilizations*, four editions of a chapter in a Thames and Hudson book *The Human Past* and various journal papers, reviews and contributions to festschrifts, published in Australia or elsewhere. In total, the latter comprised numerous smaller publications. I also wrote *The archaeology and architecture of farm buildings at Saumarez Station, Armidale, New South Wales,* published by BAR, Oxford, in 2022.

This took a lot of effort and time because, at the age of 87 and with poor eyesight, writing became increasingly difficult. It was further hampered by the conditions of aged care in which I now lived and which were restricted at times by the COVID-19 virus, which sometimes isolated me, preventing access to my records and excluding visitors from outside.

32.

Field Survey at Yanga, Near Balranald

I did a late piece of fieldwork in June 2008. This was at Yanga, near Balranald, New South Wales and was done at the request of Michael Westaway, then working for the New South Wales National Parks and Wildlife Service. It was carried out over three days, in my capacity as a Visiting Fellow at the Australian National University in Canberra and I was assisted by Beryl.

European settlement in the Balranald area originated in 1835 and Yanga became one of the largest freehold properties in Australia, a sheep and cattle station until 2005, when it was sold to the New South Wales government to be developed as a National Park. The property follows the Murrumbidgee River for about 160 kilometres. A major structure is the woolshed, with a total of nine structural events mostly dating from before about 1920. Amongst other evidence was an abandoned woolpress manufactured in Melbourne probably in the 1870s–1880s (**Figure 154**) and the use of timber slabs, although with sawn timber, in Peacock's Hut, on the property.

Figure 154. Maker's plate on a cast-iron hydraulic woolpress abandoned at Woolpress Bend on the Yanga property. The Robison engineering company operated from 1854 to 1973 but probably manufactured this press in the 1870s–1880s. Photograph in June 2008.

33.

Boyd Town Dereliction, NSW

My final piece of fieldwork was during a few days' holiday that Beryl and I took at Twofold Bay, near Eden on the New South Wales' southern coast, in February 2010. This was just before I was hospitalised for various surgeries. There we saw Ben Boyd's Tower, which was obviously well cared for.

However, I also made two visits to the ruins of the church that Boyd never completed on the top of a hill nearby and I was appalled by its condition. Obviously neglected, the brickwork was in a poor state. Dating from the 1840s, its construction was presumably abandoned when he went bankrupt. I wrote to the local government of the area about it, but they apparently did nothing because in 2022 the Internet suggested that it was still in a poor state. Cleaned up and consolidated, with the hilltop grassed and provided with several seats, it could make a pleasant tourist attraction (**Figures 155–157**).

Figure 155. Ben Boyd's Tower at Boyd Town, New South Wales. 17 February 2010. The date-stone (in Roman Numerals) is 1843.

Figure 156. Ruined tower of the unfinished church at Boyd Town, New South Wales. 18/19 February 2010.

Figure 157. Collapsing brickwork and uncontrolled vegetation in unfinished church, Boyd Town, New South Wales. 18/19 February 2010.

34.

Conclusion

My years as a Visiting Fellow at the Australian National University, a position that was renewed each year when I reported on my work during the previous year, deserve more attention than they have received above. I was attached to the Department of Archaeology and Anthropology, in the Faculty of Arts (the organisation subsequently changed), although Rhys Jones once suggested that I should be attached to the Research School archaeology department (but I did nothing about it).

In 1995, I was actually at the Humanities Research Centre, but in 1996 when I became attached to the Faculty department, Isabel McBryde had already retired as professor. Matthew Spriggs was appointed to the chair.

Other members of the department included Mary-Jane Mountain, who I remember from about 1960 when she was the curator at the Saffron Walden Museum, in England. She later worked in Papua New Guinea before coming to Canberra and at the ANU she became exceptional in her teaching and supervision of students. The staff also included Professor Colin Groves, a noted primatologist and Ian Farrington, a specialist in South American archaeology.

In addition, there was Wilfred Shawcross, a Cambridge contemporary of mine, well-known for his innovative research on a shell midden at Galatea Bay, New Zealand and appreciated by ANU students for his lecturing ability. For a while, there was also Mike Smith, concerned with Central Australian archaeological research, whose PhD was from the University of New England. The anthropology part of the ANU department seemed to have little connection with the archaeology part, although the headship of the department regularly rotated through both sections.

During the years that I was attached to the department, there was a departmental research and teaching project at the historical site of Kiandra, in the Snowy Mountains south of Canberra. This was directed by Ian Farrington, who published some of the results of the excavations, as also did Lindsay Smith, who assisted with the project, which investigated the settlement of Chinese goldminers in the past. The work was also directed by Ken Heffernan for a time.

Each year that the project continued, Beryl and I visited it to talk to the students present and to show our interest in the work. We also continued to travel during these years, visiting Central Australia in 2001 for instance, where we went to Uluru (Ayers Rock), Alice Springs and other places and even had a brief ride on a camel, but a very docile one (**Figure 158**).

Figure 158. Beryl and me and 'Bundy' the camel, Central Australia, 2001.
Antiquity 80(307), March 2006.

35.

Addendum:
Cambridge Archaeology in 1950s

On 27 and 28 February 2015, Cambridge celebrated the Centennial of the Archaeology and Anthropology Tripos. This consisted of presentations by former students and others, with several dinners. I received an email inviting me to contribute but I could not be there in person and the contribution that I sent seems to have arrived too late to be included in the printed programme. Nevertheless, I received a message assuring me that what I had sent would be read out on my behalf. As far as I know, there was no publication of the proceedings, so what I wrote follows for historical reasons. It was dated 12 February 2015 in Canberra.

My memories of Cambridge extend from 1952 to 2008 but now in my 80s I am no longer able to make the hellish journey from Australia of 20 to 30 hours and so instead I send a few cherished memories of Cambridge archaeology over 50 years ago.

I matriculated in 1956, following participation in various places in both substantial archaeological fieldwork and museum work and two years in the Royal Navy as a Coder, half of the time in a seagoing destroyer. At that time only Edinburgh and Cambridge offered full undergraduate study in archaeology, London did not offer a first degree till 1958. Edinburgh under Stuart Piggott and Richard Atkinson seemed to concentrate on European prehistory, while Cambridge's interests were far wider, as demonstrated by Grahame Clark in 1961 when he published the first edition of his book *World Prehistory*, an almost unheard-of task to undertake at that time.

However, although I came to Cambridge for archaeology, pressure from family and friends made me take the first two years of the History Tripos because employment in archaeology was then virtually non-existent and, with a history degree, one could at least get a job as a history teacher in a school. However, I rebelled in my third year and Grahame Clark allowed me to undertake third-year archaeology without doing the previous two years. I must have thought that I knew enough about archaeology to be able to do this, but I did not and my results at the end of the year, although satisfactory, were nothing like the shining glory of contemporaries Brian Fagan and Richard Wright.

Even before that final year of 1958–1959, I had become familiar with the Downing Street Department (then of Archaeology and Anthropology, although there was little interaction), largely through involvement with the Field Club (which I hope still exists).

There was the Department museum, then run by Geoffrey Bushnell, who seemed to spend a lot of his time turning off its lights, we suspected to save money but perhaps to protect its many fragile organic displays. He also distinguished himself once each year by using a spear-thrower to hurl a blackboard pointer across the then-open Downing Street courtyard: in those days there was no McDonald Institute and perhaps not even the nasty wooden huts that existed previously. In 1959, his projectile bounced off the wall in the far corner of the court, diagonally opposite to the door into 'Arc and Anth' as we called our territory.

The other academic staff and undergraduates and postgraduates were then far less numerous than they seem to be now. The main staff was headed by Professor Grahame Clark. His lectures were highly informative if rather laboured, in spite of sometimes sharing rather curious insights, as when he remarked that 'a round hut was nothing more than a long hut wrapped round a central pole'. Other senior staff were Senior Lecturers, including Glyn Daniel, who occasionally would give a brilliant lecture but was often absent in London to deal with television or publishing matters (these were the days of the famed *Animal, Vegetable and Mineral* programmes).

However, Glyn was always friendly and helpful and in 1959 organised a memorable archaeological fieldtrip of several days to South Wales, on which we all went in spite of it being only just before the examinations. There was also Charles McBurney, who really could teach and Eric Higgs who in the 1960s successfully expanded Clark's idea of economic prehistory.

In my final year, there were only 9 of us undergraduates (other than odd ones in Egyptology, Near Eastern or Anglo-Saxon studies, who had a rather separate existence). Only about half of us 9 became professional archaeologists, although for a while we had the present Queen of Denmark amongst us, who got a rather better job. As for postgraduates, there was only a handful, of whom Clark was often scathing because they took so long to finish PhDs, in fact, I doubt if some ever did.

The Arc and Anth building, often called by us 'the Arc', for short, was a depressing place, with I suspect some of the worst lecture rooms in Cambridge and internal paintwork that looked as if it dated from the beginning of the 20th Century and probably did. A back stair from the lower to the upper museum gallery even had a surviving painted warning halfway up, dating from the World War II blitz, that read 'No shelter beyond this point'. My best memory of the building, however, was of its antiquated plumbing equipment; the gents toilet, for instance, boasted an ornate toilet-roll holder of Edwardian vintage made of cast-iron, impressively inscribed 'The St Pancras Toilet Necessary'.

In those days, elderly elevated cast-iron toilet cisterns with long chains were common in Cambridge and I recollect some that had impressive names such as 'Etna', 'Vesuvius' or in one case 'Dreadnought', perhaps warning users of the potential danger if they pulled the chain with too much enthusiasm. Sadly, I cannot recollect the name of the Arc and Anth example.

I graduated in 1959 and the University surprised me by offering me a three-year job as a lone Research Assistant on an archaeomagnetic dating project, from which, because of the dilatoriness of those in charge, the only further publication to emerge was one by David Clarke and I that we produced in our 'spare time' and published in *Antiquity* in 1962. I stayed for only 2 years before going to Africa, where malaria, etc., got into my system along with an obsession with that continent and its peoples that has remained with me ever since.

So, what was my lasting impression of Cambridge Arc and Anth at that time? Frankly, it was somewhat chaotic, its lecturers nothing like as memorable as some of the more able members of the History Faculty and its organisation was sometimes poor. Thus, on the morning of my final practical examination, I suddenly discovered that an extra practical examination had been added, of which we had never been told. Somebody had merely stuck a note on the noticeboard and at the last minute.

So, when it came to my turn to be grilled by Glyn Daniel and John Evans, who was the External Examiner from the London Institute of Archaeology of which he was later the Director, I complained bitterly about this situation. Glyn merely looked at his watch, it was close to lunchtime and remarked 'They are open' and he and I retired to the nearest pub (long gone; it was known to us as 'The Bun Shop' but I think it had a more formal name). There we downed a whisky each at his expense and then returned to the practical examination.

Nevertheless, for all its faults, Arc and Anth was a magic place where we had freedom now lost from most Western universities, as governments have more and more dictated their bureaucratic nonsense with endless invasive investigations and report-writing (does anybody ever read the reports?). In those days, over half a century ago, we *talked* incessantly to each other and frequently to the academic staff.

Our favourite morning spot for us students was the top floor of 'Hawkins', a rather seedy coffee place opposite Emmanuel that vanished many years ago. There we would sit, waste time and bemoan the absence of archaeological employment, while David Clarke regaled us with his latest crop of puns. So, we had no prospects (none of us seemed to foresee the developments of the 1960s) and little or no money.

Nevertheless, we had the freedom to think and argue and sometimes agree (for instance) that Childe's beakers marching around Europe, along with the indestructible nomenclature of the Three Age System (that still impedes us, although not in more enlightened parts of the world) was all nonsense. Someday universities *might* rediscover that same chaotic freedom, freedom that sometimes allowed the lazy and stupid to get by but also allowed some others to excel.

36.
Finally

In 2019, I published *The So Pots of Central Africa: Memories of the Past* with BAR, Oxford. This was mainly based on photographs that I had taken in Borno during the 1960s but I also used all the available literature that I could find and some later photographs from Nicola Rupp, of the Johann Wolfgang Goethe University, Frankfurt, Germany and from Detlef Gronenborn, of the Mainz Museum, Germany. They had both done later fieldwork in Borno. There was a very positive but unexpected reception of the book (**Figure 159**).

Figure 159. So pot at Mudu, Borno, May 1965. Julius Tilleh as scale. Photograph by Graham Connah.

This account of archaeology at the University of New England and at the Australian National University (the latter during my 'retirement' when I was a visiting fellow there) might seem conceited, but it is only partly about me. It also records other people and many events that would otherwise have been forgotten, in this way providing a contribution to the history of two Australian universities during the later twentieth century and the beginning of the twenty-first.

John Atchison, retired from the History Department at the University of New England, has told me what Geoff Quaife, who was also formerly in the History Department and Dean of Arts for a time during the 1970s, did when he retired. He dug a hole in the garden at his house and buried all his university papers in it. This was a quick solution to the problem that I faced but a rather drastic one that I was not prepared to take.

However, there is still one matter that I should mention, this is the part played by Beryl during the years described in this account. Comments by two independent witnesses are evidence of our relationship (currently a marriage of over 60 years). Nora McMillan once remarked to me: "She loves you very much," and my sister Kathleen, after I had said that people had wondered if the marriage would last, said, "I never doubted it." Neither did I.

37.
Bibliography:
Graham Edward Connah

1954. 'Bromborough Water Mill', *Bromborough Society Twenty-First Annual Report and Balance Sheet 1953–1954*: no pagination (8 pages).

1955. 'The petrifying well at Bromborough', *Bromborough Society Twenty-Second Annual Report and Balance Sheet 1954–1955*: no pagination (5 pages).

1960. 'Roman Wirral—An index of the archaeological evidence', *Bromborough Society Twenty-Seventh Annual Report and Balance Sheet 1959–1960*: 14–24.

1962. 'An archaeological experiment with the '4c' mine detector', *Antiquity* 36: 305–306.

1962 (With D. Clarke). 'Remanent magnetism and beaker chronology', *Antiquity* 36: 206–209.

1964. *Polished stone axes in Benin.* Nigerian Department of Antiquities, Lagos, pp.32, plates 6, figs 5.

1964. (With N.F. McMillan) 'Snails and archaeology', *Antiquity* 38: 62–64.

1964 [dated 1963]. 'Archaeological research in Benin City 1961–1964', *Journal of the Historical Society of Nigeria,* 2(4): 465–477.

1965. 'Entry on Benin and Bornu'. In Calvocoressi, D. (ed.) *COWA Surveys and Bibliographies.* West Africa, Area 11, No. 3: COWA Survey pp. 8–9.

1965. 'Excavations at Knap Hill', *Wiltshire Archaeological Magazine* 60: 1–23.

1966. 'Progress report', In *Northern History Research Scheme: First Interim Report*, Zaria, Nigeria, pp. 11–21.

1966. 'Summary of research in Benin City and in Bornu', *West African Archaeological Newsletter* 5: 22–25.

1967. 'New light on the Benin City walls', *Journal of the Historical Society of Nigeria,* 3(4): 593–609.

n.d. [1967]. *A map of the Benin City walls*. Federal Department of Antiquities, Nigeria.

1967. 'Progress report on archaeological work in Bornu 1964–1966 with particular reference to the excavations at Daima mound', In *Northern History Research Scheme: Second Interim Report*, Zaria, Nigeria, pp. 20–31.

1967. 'Classic' excavation in North-East Nigeria', *Illustrated London News*, 14 October: 42–44.

1967. 'Radiocarbon dates for Daima, N.E. Nigeria', *Journal of the Historical Society of Nigeria* 3(4): 741–742.

1967. 'Radiocarbon dates for Daima, N.E. Nigeria', *West African Archaeological Newsletter* 6: 23–24.

1967. 'Premier Colloque International d'Archéologie Africaine, Fort Lamy 11–17 December 1966', *West African Archaeological Newsletter,* 6: 46–51.

1967. 'An apology for 'culture', *West African Archaeological Newsletter,* 7: 13–15.

1968. 'Radiocarbon dates for Benin City and further dates for Daima, N.E. Nigeria', *Journal of the Historical Society of Nigeria,* 4(2): 313–320.

1968. 'A West African Archaeological Journal: The necessity and the possibilities', *West African Archaeological Newsletter* 9: 63–68.

1969. 'Settlement mounds of the firki: The reconstruction of a lost society', *Ibadan* 26: 48–62.

1969. 'Three lectures on Nigerian prehistory', In Shaw, T. (ed.) *Lectures on Nigerian prehistory and archaeology*, Ibadan: Ibadan University Press, pp. 30–36 & 47–61.

1969. (With F. Willett) 'Pottery making in the village of Use near Benin City', *Baessler Archiv* (Berlin), 17: 133–149.

1969. 'Archaeological work in Bornu 1964–1966 with particular reference to the excavations at Daima mound', *Actes du Premier Colloque International d'Archeologie Africaine, Fort-Lamy (République du Tchad) 11–16 décembre 1966*, pp. 112–124.

1969. 'Excavations at Daima, N.E. Nigeria', *Palaeoecology of Africa,* 4: 131–132.

1969. 'Entry on current research'. In Calvocoressi, D. (ed.) *COWA Surveys and Bibliographies*. West Africa, Area 11, No. 4: COWA Survey pp. 12–13.

1969. 'Radiocarbon dating for Knap Hill', *Antiquity* 43: 304–305.

1969. Assistant Editor. *West African Archaeological Newsletter,* 11.

1970. 'Radiocarbon dating and laboratory examinations for Knap Hill', *Wiltshire Archaeological Magazine* (volume and page numbers unknown).

1970. 'Recent contributions to Bornu chronology', *West African Journal of Archaeology,* 1: 55–60.

1970. 'Precursors of Daima?', *West African Archaeological Newsletter,* 12: 91–92.

1970. Assistant Editor. *West African Archaeological Newsletter* 12.

1971. 'The archaeology of Benin City'. In Fagg, A. (ed.) *Papers presented to the 4th Conference of West African Archaeologists, Jos 1971.* Federal Department of Antiquities, Jos Museum, Nigeria, pp. 14–18.

1971. (With S.P. Bohrer) 'Pathology in 700-year-old Nigerian bones. Query: Sickle cell infarcts', *Radiology* 98(3): 581–584.

1971. Assistant Editor. *West African Journal of Archaeology* 1.

1972. 'Archaeology in Benin', *Journal of African History* 13(1): 25–38.

1972. 'Method and ritual in excavation'. A review article of Alexander, J. 1970. *The directing of archaeological excavations.* John Baker, London. *West African Journal of Archaeology,* 2: 128–130.

1972. 'Book review of Shinnie', P.L. (ed.) 1971. *The African Iron Age.* Clarendon Press, Oxford. *The Antiquaries Journal,* 52(2): 376–377.

1972. 'Excavations at Daima, N.E. Nigeria', *Actes de 6ᵉ session, Congrès panafricain de préhistoire, Dakar, 1967,* pp. 146–147.

1972. Assistant Editor. *West African Journal of Archaeology* 2.

1973. 'A milestone in African prehistory', A review article of Clark, J.D. 1970. *The prehistory of Africa.* Thames and Hudson, London. *West African Journal of Archaeology* 3: 253–255.

1973. Assistant Editor. *West African Journal of Archaeology* 3.

1975. *The archaeology of Benin.* Clarendon Press, Oxford, pp. 284, plates 49, figs 66, tables 26.

1975. Two chapters in Shaw, T. (ed.) *Discovering Nigeria's past.* Oxford University Press, Ibadan, pp. 27–38 & 92–99.

1975. 'Current research at the Department of Prehistory and Archaeology, University of New England', *Australian Archaeology,* 3: 28–31.

1976. 'The Daima sequence and the prehistoric chronology of the Lake Chad region of Nigeria', *Journal of African History,* 17(3): 321–352.

1976. 'Archaeology at the University of New England, 1975–6', *Australian Archaeology,* 5: 1–6.

1976. (With P. Emmerson and J. Stanley) 'Is there a place for the proton magnetometer in Australian field archaeology?', *Mankind,* 10(3): 151–155.

1977. 'Wool, water and settlement: The archaeological landscape of Saumarez Station', *Armidale and District Historical Society Journal,* 20: 117–127.

1977. (With I. Davidson and M.J. Rowland) 'Prehistoric settlement'. In Lea, D.A.M., Pigram, J.J.J. and Greenwood, L. (eds) *An atlas of New England,* Vols 1 and 2, Armidale: University of New England, Vol. 1: p. 15 and Vol. 2: pp. 127–136.

1977. 'Archaeological techniques and evidence'. In Stanton, G.R. (ed.) *For teachers of ancient history: Proceedings of a conference held at the University of New England, 1–3 May 1976,* Sydney: New South Wales Department of Education, pp. 1–7.

1978. 'Aborigine and settler: Archaeological air photography', *Antiquity* 52: 95–99 + 10 plates.

1978. 'Recent ethnographic and archaeological fieldwork in Borno', *Nyame Akuma,*13: 14–22.

1978. (With M.J. Rowland and J. Oppenheimer) *Captain Richards' house at Winterbourne: A study in historical archaeology,* Armidale: University of New England, pp.96, plates 25, figs 21, tables 1.

1978. (With J. Stanley) 'Magnetic evidence of an Aboriginal burial ground at Forster, N.S.W', *A collection of papers presented to ANZAAS 1977.* Memoirs of the Victorian Archaeological Survey, Vol. 2, pp. 37–50.

1979. 'Borno revisited: ethnographic and archaeological fieldwork in 1978', *Zaria Archaeological Papers,* Centre for Nigerian Cultural Studies, Ahmadu Bello University, Zaria, Nigeria. (Volume number and pagination unknown).

1979. (With D. Clarke) 'Remanent magnetism and beaker chronology', 1962 paper reprinted in *Analytical Archaeologist: Collected papers of David L. Clarke,* London: Academic Press.

1980. 'An experiment that failed? Water-power in 19th-century New England', *Australian Society for Historical Archaeology: Newsletter,* 10(2): 18–21.

1981. 'Man and a Lake', *2000 ans d'histoire africaine: Le sol, la parole et l'écrit: Mélanges en hommage à Raymond Mauny.* Société française d'histoire d'outre-mer, Paris: Tome I, pp. 161–178.

1981. *Three thousand years in Africa: Man and his environment in the Lake Chad region of Nigeria.* Cambridge University Press, Cambridge, pp.268, figs 100, histograms 14, tables 16.

1981. (With D.R. Horton) 'Man and megafauna at Reddestone Creek, near Glen Innes, Northern New South Wales', *Australian Archaeology,* 13: 35–52.

1982. (With J. Jemkur) 'Prospecting the 3000 B.P. barrier: Borno 1981', *Nyame Akuma,* 20: 35–43.

1983. 'Stamp collecting or increasing understanding?: The dilemma of historical archaeology', *Australian Journal of Historical Archaeology* 1: 15–21.

1983. Editor. *Australian Journal of Historical Archaeology* 1, pp.89, figs 29, tables 1.

1983. Editor. *Australian field archaeology: A guide to techniques.* Australian Institute of Aboriginal Studies, Canberra, pp. viii + 182, figs 179, tables 22.

1983. (With A. Jones) 'Photographing Australian prehistoric sites from the air'. In Connah, G. (ed.) *Australian field archaeology: A guide to techniques,* Canberra: Australian Institute of Aboriginal Studies, pp. 78–81.

1983. (With A. Jones) 'Aerial archaeology in Australia', *Aerial Archaeology* 9: i–vi, 1–23.

1983. 'Comment on communications by B. Fagan and J.E.G. Sutton concerning the presentation of archaeological evidence', *Journal of African History,* 24: 536–537.

1983. 'Some contributions of archaeology to the study of the history of Borno'. In Usman, B. and Alkali, N. (eds.) *Studies in the history of pre-colonial Borno.* Northern Nigerian Publishing Company, Zaria, pp.1–15. [Published without the author's consent or knowledge, probably pirated from other writings of his and heavily edited.]

1984. 'Archaeological exploration in southern Borno', *African Archaeological Review,* 2: 153–171.

1984. Book review of Clark, J.D. (ed.) 1982. *The Cambridge History of Africa;* Vol. 1: *From the earliest times to c.500 B.C.* Cambridge: Cambridge University Press, *Africa* 54(3): 112–113.

1984. Book review of McIntosh, S.K. and McIntosh, R.J. 1980. *Prehistoric investigations in the region of Jenne, Mali: A study in the development of urbanism in the Sahel*; Part i: *Archaeological and historical background and the excavations at Jenne-Jeno*; Part ii: *The regional survey and conclusions.* BAR International Series 89(i) and 89(ii), Oxford. *Africa* 54(4): 89–90.

1984. Book review of Eades, J.S. *The Yoruba today.* Cambridge University Press, Cambridge. *Mankind* 14(3): 231–232.

1984. Editor. *Australian Journal of Historical Archaeology* 2, pp.89, figs 52, tables 4.

1985. 'Agricultural intensification and sedentism in the firki of N.E. Nigeria'. In Farrington, I.S. (ed.) *Prehistoric intensive agriculture in the tropics*, BAR International Series 232, Oxford, pp. 765–785.

1985. 'Comment on Agorsah, E.K. Archaeological implications of traditional house construction among the Nchumuru of northern Ghana', *Current Anthropology* 26(1): 108–109.

1985. Editor. *Australian Journal of Historical Archaeology* 3, pp.84, figs 41, tables 2.

1986. 'Historical reality: Archaeological reality. Excavations at Regentville, Penrith, New South Wales, 1985', *Australian Journal of Historical Archaeology* 4: 29–42.

1986. Editor. *Australian Journal of Historical Archaeology* 4, pp.85, figs 77.

1987. *African civilisations: Precolonial cities and states in tropical Africa: An archaeological perspective*, Cambridge: Cambridge University Press, pp.260, figs 55. (In hardcover and paperback, paperback reprinted 10 times by 1999).

1987. *The purposes of archaeology.* Inaugural lecture, University of New England, 13 October 1986, Armidale: University of New England, 16 pages.

1987. Book review of McGowan, A. 1985. *Archaeological investigations at Risdon Cove Historic Site 1978–1980.* National Parks and Wildlife Service, Tasmania. *Australian Archaeology* 24: 78–79.

1987. Editor. *Australian Journal of Historical Archaeology* 5, pp.85, figs 60, tables 7.

1988. *'Of the hut I builded': The archaeology of Australia's history*, Melbourne: Cambridge University Press, pp.176, figs 91.

1988. Editor. *Australian Journal of Historical Archaeology* 6, pp.108, figs 76, tables 5.

1989. 'Kibiro revisited: An archaeological reconnaissance in south-western Uganda, 1989', *Nyame Akuma,* 32: 46–54.

1989. (With S.J. Freeth) 'A commodity problem in prehistoric Borno', *Sahara* 2: 7–20.

1989. American historical archaeology and the search for 'meaning', Book review of Leone, M.P. and Potter, P.B. Jr (eds) 1988. *The recovery of meaning: historical archaeology in the eastern United States.* Washington (DC): Smithsonian Institution Press, *Antiquity,* 63: 370–372.

1990. 'Archaeology in Western Uganda 1990', *Nyame Akuma,* 34: 38–45.

1990. (With E. Kamuhangire and A. Piper) 'Salt production at Kibiro', *Azania* 25: 27–39 and plates 1–6.

1990. Book review of Barbour, J. and Wandibba, S. (eds) 1989. *Kenyan pots and potters*, Nairobi: Oxford University Press, *Azania,* 25: 102–104.

1991. 'The salt of Bunyoro: Seeking the origins of an African kingdom', *Antiquity,* 65: 479–494.

1993. *The archaeology of Australia's history.* Paperback edition, Melbourne: Cambridge University Press, pp.176, figs 91. (Originally published in 1988.)

1993. Japanese language edition of *African civilizations.* Kawade Shobo. [Originally published by Cambridge: Cambridge University Press, 1987.]

1993. Book review of Shinnie, P.L. and Kense, F.J. 1989. *Archaeology of Gonja, Ghana: Excavations at Daboya.* Calgary University Press, Calgary. *Journal of African History,* 34: 505–506.

1994. 'Archaeological field research in the Western Rift Valley of Uganda', *African Studies Association of Australia and the Pacific: Review and Newsletter,* 16(2): 16–19.

1994. 'Handraulic archaeology at Lake Innes House', *Australasian Society for Historical Archaeology Newsletter* 24(3): 6–8.

1994. Editor. *Archaeology and the historical artefact.* Department of Archaeology and Palaeoanthropology, University of New England, pp.59, figs 71, table 1.

1995. *Lake Innes House, Port Macquarie.* Department of Archaeology and Palaeoanthropology, University of New England, for NSW National Parks and Wildlife Service. (Guide leaflet).

1995. Africa: Precolonial achievement: 10–12 June 1995. (Report on the conference), *Humanities Research Centre Bulletin* (Australian National University), 79: 5–9.

1995. 'Africa: Precolonial achievement. A conference held 10–12 June 1995 at the Humanities Research Centre, Canberra: Australian National University', *Australian Historical Association Bulletin,* 81: 35–9.

1995. Book review of Kenderine, S. and Jeffery, B. (eds) n.d. *Muddy waters: Proceedings of the first conference on the submerged and terrestrial archaeology of historic shipping on the River Murray, Echuca, 21–23 September*

1992. State Heritage Branch, Department of Environment and Natural Resources, Adelaide. *The Great Circle,* 17(1): 70–71.

1995. 'Early farming communities on the eastern shores of Lake Albert and along the lower Victoria Nile (Summary)', *Azania,* 29–30: 315.

1996. *Kibiro: The salt of Bunyoro, past and present.* Memoir 13, London: British Institute in Eastern Africa, pp.224, figs 159, tables 34.

1996. The archaeology of European settlement in Australia. Benin. Two entries in Fagan, B.M. (ed.) *The Oxford companion to archaeology.* New York: Oxford University Press, pp. 75–76, 751.

1996. 'Welcome back: The return of the Panafrican Congress', *African Archaeological Review,* 13(4): 261–5.

1996. 'A chronological sequence for the Ugandan shores of Lake Albert'. In Pwiti, G. and Soper, R. (eds) *Aspects of African archaeology: Papers from the 10th Congress of the PanAfrican Association for Prehistory and Related Studies.* Harare: University of Zimbabwe, pp. 533–541.

1996 [dated 1995]. (With N.F. McMillan) 'Mollusca utilisation in prehistoric Borno: A case of human preference?', *Sahara,* 7: 29–38.

1996 [dated 1994]. 'Bagot's Mill: Genesis and Revelation in an archaeological research project', *Australasian Historical Archaeology,* 12: 3–55.

1996 [dated 1994]. Editor. *Australasian Historical Archaeology* 12, pp.56, figs 87, tables 11.

1997. 'The cultural and chronological context of Kibiro, Uganda', *African Archaeological Review* (Plenum Publishing Corporation, New York), 14(1): 25–67.

1997. 'Development of states in Sub-Saharan Africa'. In Vogel, J.O. (ed.) *Encyclopedia of precolonial Africa: Archaeology, history, languages, cultures and environments,* Walnut Creek, California: AltaMira Press, pp. 457–61.

1997. Editor. *The archaeology of Lake Innes House: Investigating the visible evidence 1993–1995.* Published by Connah, Canberra, for the New South Wales National Parks and Wildlife Service, pp.45, figs 47.

1997. 'The purposes of archaeology'. (Reprinted Inaugural Lecture, University of New England, 1986). *Australian Archaeology,* 45: 48–53.

1998. 'Static image, dynamic reality'. In Connah, G. (ed.) *Transformations in Africa: Essays on Africa's later past.* Leicester University Press (Cassell Academic, London), pp. 1–13.

1998. Editor. *Transformations in Africa: Essays on Africa's later past*. Leicester University Press (London: Cassell Academic), pp.xvi+255, figs 36, tables 6.

1998. 'The archaeology of frustrated ambition: An Australian case-study', *Historical Archaeology,* 32(2): 7–27.

1998. (With I. Davidson and I. McBryde) 'Archaeology and Palaeoanthropology at UNE: Prehistory and history, 1959–1999'. In Ryan, J.S. (ed) *The Arts from New England: University provision and outreach 1928–1998.* Armidale: University of New England, pp. 194–207.

1998. 'Resource exploitation and population aggregation: The case of Kibiro'. In Sinclair, P. (ed.) *The development of urbanism from a global perspective.* Department of Archaeology and Ancient History, Sweden: Uppsala University. Electronic publication
http://www.arkeologi.uu.se/Forskning/Publikationer/Digital/Development_of_Urbanism/

1999 [dated 1998]. 'Pattern and purpose in historical archaeology', *Australasian Historical Archaeology,* 16: 3–7.

1999. 'Charles Thurstan Shaw'. In Murray, T. (ed) *The Great Archaeologists*, Vol. II, Santa Barbara, California: ABC-Clio, pp. 727–741.

1999. 'The Lake Innes Project 1999', *Australasian Society for Historical Archaeology Newsletter,* 29(3): 3–5.

1999 [dated 1998]. Book review of Fletcher, R. 1995. *The limits of settlement growth: A theoretical outline.* Cambridge: Cambridge University Press, *Australasian Historical Archaeology,* 16: 94.

2000. 'African city walls. A neglected source?'. In Anderson, D.M. and Rathbone, R. eds) *Africa's urban past.* James Currey, Oxford, pp. 36–51.

2000. 'Contained communities in tropical Africa'. In Tracy, J.D. (ed.) *City walls: The urban enceinte in global perspective.* Cambridge: Cambridge University Press, pp. 19–45.

2000. 'The voice of the artefact: Museums as historical sources'. In Macknight, C. (ed.) *Historians and museums: New sites of knowledge. Tasmanian Historical Studies,* 7(1): 5–20.

2000. 'The Lake Innes Project: Past, present, future', *Australasian Society for Historical Archaeology Newsletter,* 30(4): 6–7.

2000. Book review of Knapp, A.B., Pigott, V.C. and Herbert, E.W. (eds) 1998. *Social approaches to an industrial past: The archaeology and anthropology of mining*, London and New York: Routledge. *Australian Geographical Studies* 38(2): 235–237.

2000. Book review of McIntosh, S.K. (ed.) 1999. *Beyond Chiefdoms: Pathways to complexity in Africa.* Cambridge University Press, Cambridge. *Journal of Anthropological Research,* 56(4): 592–593.

2000. '19th-century ironworkers in Central Africa'. Book review of Kriger, C.E. 1999. *Pride of Men: Ironworking in 19th century West Central Africa.* Heinemann, Portsmouth, NH et al. *African Studies Review and Newsletter* (Australasia), 22(2): 49–51.

2001. *African civilizations: An archaeological perspective,* Second Edition, Cambridge: Cambridge University Press, pp.340, figs 75.

2001. 'The Lake Innes Estate: Privilege and servitude in nineteenth-century Australia', *World Archaeology,* 33(1): 137–154.

2001. 'A hoard of stone beads near Lake Chad, Nigeria' *Beads. Journal of the Society of Bead researchers,* 8–9: 35–43 and Plates VA & VB.

2001. *Rediscovering Africa.* The Fourth Museum of Antiquities Maurice Kelly Lecture, delivered at the University of New England, Armidale, 24 October 2000, pp.30, figs 15.

2001. 'Writing Africa's archaeological past: Who writes for whom?', *The Australasian Review of African Studies,* 23(1): 32–37.

2001. 'The Lake Innes Project 2001', *Australasian Society for Historical Archaeology Newsletter,* 31(4): 5–7.

2001. Book review of Ehret, C. 1998. *An African Classical Age: Eastern and Southern Africa in world history, 1000 B.C. to 400 A.D.* University Press of Virginia, Charlottesville and James Currey, Oxford. *Journal of World History* 12(1): 205–208.

2002. (With D. Pearson). 'Artefact of Empire: The tale of a gun', *Historical Archaeology,* 36(2): 58–70.

2002. 'Twenty years on', *Australasian Historical Archaeology,* 20: 1–3.

2002. 'Lake Innes Estate, Australia'. In Orser, C.E. Jr (ed.) *Encyclopedia of historical archaeology,* London: Routledge, pp. 307–308.

2002. 'Obituary: Desmond Clark (1916–2002)', *Australasian Review of African Studies* 24(1): 4–5.

2002. Book review of Phillipson, D.W. 2000. *Archaeology at Aksum, Ethiopia, 1993–7* (2 volumes). British Institute in Eastern Africa and Society of Antiquaries of London, London. *Antiquity* 76: 275–276.

2002. 'Modelling the African past'. Book review of Ehret, C. 2002. *The civilisations of Africa: A history to 1800*. James Curry, Oxford. *Australasian Review of African Studies,* 24(2): 70–72.

2003. 'Problem orientation in Australian historical archaeology', *Historical Archaeology,* 37(1): 146–158.

2003. 'Images of Africa', (The Mulvaney Lecture for 2003, School of Archaeology and Anthropology, Australian National University) *Australasian Review of African Studies,* 25(1): 26–37.

2003. Book review of Holl, A.F.C. 2002. *The Land of Houlouf: Genesis of a Chadic polity, 1900 BC–AD 1800.* Memoirs of the Museum of Anthropology, University of Michigan, Number 35, Ann Arbor, Michigan. *African Archaeological Review* 20(3): 171–174.

2003. (With S.G.H. Daniels). Mining the archives: A pottery sequence for Borno, Nigeria. *Journal of African Archaeology* 1(1): 39–76.

2004. *Forgotten Africa: An introduction to its archaeology,* London and New York: Routledge, xiv+193 pages, 67 figures. Published in hardback, paperback, and e-Book.

2004. 'Publish and be damned?' In Smith, L., Rose, P., Wahida, G. and Wahida, S. (eds) *Fifty years in the archaeology of Africa: Themes in archaeological theory and practice. Papers in honour of John Alexander. Azania* Special Volume 39: 325–336, Nairobi: British Institute in Eastern Africa.

2004. 'Potential and realisation in the archaeology of Benin City'. In Murray, T. (ed.) *Archaeology from Australia.* Melbourne: Australian Scholarly Publishing.

2004. Book review of Damaris Bairstow. *A million pounds, a million acres. The pioneer settlement of the Australian Agricultural Company.* Published by the author, Cremorne, NSW, 2003; xiv + 418 pages, 10 maps, 4 plans, 19 black-and-white plates. *Australasian Historical Archaeology,* 22: 90–91.

2004. Book review of Reid, A.M. and Lane, P.J. (eds) *African historical archaeologies.* Kluwer Academic and Plenum Publishers, New York, 2004, 408 pages, 82 figures, 23 tables. *Journal of Field Archaeology* 29 (3–4): 477–479.

2004. Book review of Mitchell, P., Haour, A. and Hobart, J. (eds) *Researching Africa's past: New contributions from British archaeologists.* Proceedings of a meeting held at St Hugh's College, Oxford, Saturday, 20 April 2002. Oxford University School of Archaeology Monograph No. 57, Oxford, United Kingdom: Oxford University School of Archaeology, 2003, viii + 152 pages. *Journal of African Archaeology* 2 (2): 277–279.

2005. [dated 2004] 'Writing Africa's archaeological past', *Nyame Akuma,* 62: 78–80.

2005. Chapter 10. Holocene Africa. In Scarre, C. (ed.) *The human past: World prehistory & the development of human societies.* Thames and Hudson, London, pp. 350–391.

2005. 'The Bromborough Society over fifty years ago', *The Bromborough Society 72nd Annual Report and Balance Sheet 2004–2005.* (Bromborough, Merseyside. United Kingdom.)

2005. 'Knowing Africa's archaeological past'. Book review of Stahl, A.B. (ed.) *African archaeology: A critical introduction.* Blackwell, Oxford. *Cambridge Archaeological Journal* 15(2): 270–273.

2006. 'Retrospect', *Antiquity* 80: 173–184.

2006. Foreword. In Kriger, C.E. *Cloth in West African history.* Lanham, MD, USA, pp. xiii–xvi.

2006. Book review of Macfarlane, I., Mountain, M.J. and Paton, R. (eds) 2005. *Many Exchanges: Archaeology, history, community and the work of Isabel McBryde* (Aboriginal History Monograph 11). Aboriginal History Inc., Canberra. *Antiquity* 80: 1019–1020.

2006. *Unbekanntes Afrika: Archäologische Entdeckungen auf dem Schwarzen Kontinent.* Konrad Theiss, Stuttgart. [German edition of *Forgotten Africa: An introduction to its archaeology*, London: Routledge, 2004. Translated by Beate Dillmann-Gräsing.]

2007. *The same under a different sky? A country estate in nineteenth-century New South Wales.* British Archaeological Reports, International Series 1625, Oxford, UK, ix+269 pages, 174 figures, 48 tables.

2007. 'Historical archaeology in Africa: An appropriate concept?' *African Archaeological Review* 24(1/2): 35–40.

2007. 'A pottery corpus for Daima', *Journal of African Archaeology,* 5(2): 245–270.

2007. (With A. Brooks). 'A hierarchy of servitude: Ceramics at Lake Innes Estate, New South Wales', *Antiquity,* 81: 133–147.

2008. *Afrique oubliée: Une introduction à l'archéologie du continent.* Traduit de l'anglais par Anne Haour et Céline Moguen, L'Harmattan, Paris. [French translation of Connah, G. 2004. *Forgotten Africa: An introduction to its archaeology,* London: Routledge.]

2008. 'Urbanism and the archaeological visibility of African complex societies', *Journal of African Archaeology,* 6(2): 233–241.

2008. [dated 2007]. 'Creating the canon: Materialising Australian historical archaeology', *Australasian Historical Archaeology,* 25: 105–107.

2009. Book review of Barham, L. and Mitchell, P. 2008. *The first Africans: African archaeology from the earliest toolmakers to most recent foragers.* Cambridge: Cambridge University Press, *Antiquity,* 83: 225–226.

2009. Paperback reprint of 1981. *Three thousand years in Africa: Man and his environment in the Lake Chad region of Nigeria.* Cambridge: Cambridge University Press.

2009. Chapter 10. Holocene Africa. In Scarre, C. (ed.) *The human past: World prehistory & the development of human societies,* 2nd Edition, Thames and Hudson, London, pp. 350–391.

2009. 'Taking the pulse of African archaeology: The Society of Africanist Archaeologists 19th Biennial Conference', Germany: Frankfurt am Main, 8–11 September 2008. *Azania: Archaeological Research in Africa,* 44(1): 131–135.

2009. 'Lake Innes: Identifying socioeconomic status in the archaeological record', *Historical Archaeology,* 43(3): 82–94.

2009. *Africa dimenticata: L'archeologia del continente africano.* Edizioni Arkeios, Roma, 247 pages, 67 figures, ISBN 978-88-86495-94-3 (Paperback). Italian edition of Connah, G. 2004. *Forgotten Africa: An introduction to its archaeology,* London: Routledge.

2009. 'Paul Ashbee 23 June 1918-19th August 2009: An appreciation', *Antiquity,* 83 (No. 322): Website Bulletin, one page. http://antiquity.ac.uk/tributes/ashbee.html.

2010. *Writing about archaeology.* New York: Cambridge University Press, xiii + 210 pages, 31 figures, ISBN 978-0-521-86850-1 (Hardback) ISBN 978-0-521-68851-2 (Paperback).

2010. 'Urbanisation: Pre-Colonial'. In Irele, F.A. and Jeyifo, B. (eds.) *Encyclopedia of African thought.* New York and Oxford: Oxford University Press, pagination unknown.

2010. (With D. Pearson). 'Battlefield casualty: The archaeology of a captured gun', *Journal of Conflict Archaeology,* 5: 231–256.

2010. Book review of Paterson, A.G. *The lost legions: Culture contact in colonial Australia.* AltaMira, Lanham (MD). *Antiquity,* 84: 272–273.

2011. *Prelude: Growing up in the Middle of the Twentieth Century*, Canberra: Privately published, ISBN 978-0-646-56855-3, 133 pages, 95 figures. A personal memoir.

2011. Book review of Lawrence, S. and Davies, P. *An Archaeology of Australia Since 1788.* Springer, New York, ISBN 978-1-4419-7484-6. *Australasian Historical Archaeology,* 29: pagination unknown.

2011. *Fragments of a Vanished Dream: A Visit to Lake Innes House.* New South Wales: Privately published guidebook for National Parks and Wildlife Service, Canberra, ISBN 978-0-646-55945-2, 10 pages, 10 figures.

2011. 'Early states and state formation in Africa'. In Spier, T. (ed.), *Oxford Bibliographies Online: African Studies*, New York: Oxford University Press. [Consisting of 128 annotated references with section introductions, totalling 9467 words.] http://www.oxfordbibliographies.com/view/document/obo-9780199846733/obo-9780199846733-0047.xml (Cited 19.12.12).

2012. 'West African kingdoms: Benin' and 'Australia and New Guinea: the archaeology of European settlement in Australia'. In Silberman, N.A. (ed.) *The Oxford Companion to Archaeology*, Second Edition, pagination unknown. New York: Oxford University Press.

2013. 'Archaeological practice in Africa: a historical perspective'. In Mitchell, P. and Lane, P. (ed.) *The Oxford handbook of African archaeology,* 15–36, Oxford: Oxford University Press.

2013. 'Holocene Africa'. In Scarre, C. (ed.) *The human past: world prehistory and the development of human societies*, Third Edition, 350–91. London: Thames and Hudson.

2013. Book review of: S.A. Dueppen's *Egalitarian revolution in the savanna: the origins of a West African political system.* Equinox, Sheffield, UK. *Journal of Anthropological Research* 69(1), pagination unknown.

2013. 'Aksum at the cutting edge'. Book review of: D.W. Phillipson's *Foundations of an African civilisation: Aksum and the Northern Horn, 1000 BC-AD 1300.* James Currey, Suffolk, England. *Journal of African History* 54(2), 288–9.

2013. *África desconhecida: uma introdução à sua arqueologia.* Editora da Universidade de São Paulo, São Paulo, Brazil. Translated by Carlos Magnavita, Johann Wolfgang Goethe Universität, Frankfurt am Main, Germany. Portuguese translation of my 2004 book *Forgotten Africa: an introduction to its archaeology,* London: Routledge.

2013. Pearson, D. and Connah, G. 2013. 'Retrieving the cultural biography of a gun', *Journal of Conflict Archaeology,* 8(1), 41–73.

2014. Book review of *The Power of Walls: Fortifications in Ancient North-eastern Africa. Proceedings of the International Workshop held at the University of Cologne 4–7 August 2011*, edited by F. Jesse and C. Vogel. Köln: Heinrich-Barth-Institut, 2013. *Azania: archaeological research in Africa.* 49(2): 273–5.

2015. *African civilizations: an archaeological perspective,* Third Edition, New York: Cambridge University Press, xiii+412 pages, 91 figures. Substantial revision and updating of previous editions (1987 and 2001) and 3 additional chapters. Work commenced in January 2012 and was submitted to a publisher in 2015.

2015. 'Cambridge archaeology in the 1950s'. Written to be read (in my absence) at an anniversary conference in the Department of Archaeology, University of Cambridge. Unknown, if published.

2016. With Pearson, D. 2016. *Qasr Ibrim House 1037: Resurrecting an excavation,* Oxford, British Archaeological Reports, International Series 2821, 96 pages, 52 figures, 3 tables. ISBN 978 1 4073 1560 7.

2016. Shaw, (Charles) Thurstan (1914–2013), archaeologist. *Dictionary of National Biography,* Oxford: Oxford University Press. Pagination is currently unknown.

2016. Book Review: Rowan Patel 2016. *The windmills and watermills of Wirral: A historical survey*, Birkenhead: Countyvise Ltd, *The Eastham Archivist* 25: 12. [An electronic newsletter in Merseyside, United Kingdom.]

2017. A world of clay. (A study of archaeological clay figurines from North-Eastern Nigeria and of comparable material from elsewhere in Africa). In N. Rupp et al. (eds), 111–120. *Winds of change. Festscrift for Professor Peter Breunig, Johann Wolfgang Goethe Universität, Frankfurt.* Bonn, Dr. Rudolf Habelt Verlag, Frankfurter Archäologische Schriften 35.

2018. The African Holocene. Chapter 11 in Scarre, C. (ed.) 344–387. *The human past,* 4th Edition, London, Thames and Hudson. (I also contributed to this chapter [previously numbered Chapter 10] to all three previous editions.)

2018. The catalyst. In K-J. Lindholm and A. Ekblom (eds). *The Resilience of Heritage: Festschrift for Professor Paul Sinclair, Sweden: Uppsala University,* Pp. 31–33, Uppsala University Press.

2019. *From Cambridge to Lake Chad: Life in archaeology 1956–1971,* Oxford: Archaeopress.

2019. *The So pots of Central Africa: Memories of the past,* Oxford: BAR International Series 2938.

2019. *Vestiges of the past: Excavating Saumarez Old Homestead.* Connah, Canberra. (52 copies printed).

2021. *The archaeology and architecture of farm buildings at Saumarez Station, Armidale, New South Wales.* BAR International Series S3067, Pp. 148, 159 figures. Oxford.

2022. 'Urban and state synoecism in African societies'. In M. Gehler and R. Rollinger, (eds) *Empires to be remembered. Ancient worlds through modern times,* pp. 399–410. Springer VS, Wiesbaden.

2022. Chapter 13. *Africa.* In Scarre, C. and Stone, T. (eds) *The human past: Essentials.* Thames & Hudson, London.

2022. Book review of Peter Breunig and Gabrielle Franke. *Archaeological Map of Northeast Nigeria.* Frankfurt am Main. Africa Magna Verlag. 2019, pp. 334. *Journal of African Archaeology* 20 (2022): 135–136.

2022. In cooperation with B.M. Fagan. 'Research in retrospect: The Animal Bones from Daima, Northeast Nigeria', *Journal of African Archaeology,* 20 (2022), 125–133.

2023. *A person to remember: Nora Fisher McMillan 16 March 1908–23 August 2003,* Privately published by Connah, Canberra, Australia.

www.ingramcontent.com/pod-product-compliance
Lightning Source LLC
Chambersburg PA
CBHW060459290526
45791CB00001B/181